Once Upon a Crime...

Using stories, simulations, and mock trials to explore justice and citizenship in elementary school

Wanda Cassidy and Ruth Yates

DETSELIG
ENTERPRISES LTD

Detselig Enterprises Ltd.
Calgary, Alberta

Once Upon a Crime . . .

Simon Fraser University

Cataloguing in Publication Information

Cassidy, Wanda, 1950-
    Once upon a crime : using stories, simulations, and mock trials to
explore justice and citizenship in elementary school / Wanda Cassidy, Ruth Yates.

Includes bibliographical references
ISBN 1-55059-298-X

    1. Mock trials – Study and teaching (Elementary) 2. Law – Study and
teaching (Elementary) 3. Justice – Study and teaching (Elementary).
I. Yates, Ruth, 1944- II. Title

KE3883.L3C39 2005   372.83'2044   C2005-902660-X
KF4208.5.L3C38 2005

Detselig Enterprises Ltd.
210, 1220 Kensington Road NW
Calgary, Alberta, Canada T2N 3P5

Phone: (403) 283-0900
Fax: (403) 283-6947
email: temeron@telusplanet.net
website: www.temerondetselig.com

Detselig Enterprises Ltd. acknowledges the support of the Alberta Foundation for the
Arts (AFA) for our publishing program. We also acknowledge the financial support of
the Government of Canada through the Book Publishing Industry Development
Program (BPIDP) for our publishing activities.

ISBN 1-55059-298-x
SAN 115-0324
Printed in Canada

Preface

This book has been several years in the making. Several years ago, we developed a series of fairytale mock trials for Law Day in Vancouver – an annual event sponsored by the Law Courts and the Law Courts Education Society as a way to inform the public about the workings of the courts and legal system. Our trial of Goldilocks and the Three Bears, performed by elementary students in costume and presided over by a Supreme Court Justice, turned out to be an extremely popular event with children and adults alike. We received scores of letters from teachers, parents, students, and participating judges and lawyers expressing their appreciation for the mock trial experience and suggesting we find some way to bring the experience into classrooms.

Later, as we worked with practising and prospective teachers in the law education courses we offer through the Faculty of Education at Simon Fraser University in Burnaby, BC, we found that mock trials and other conflict resolution activities provided participants with a wonderful opportunity to learn about legal concepts and principles. The stories that formed the basis of these trials were familiar to all: *The Three Little Pigs* and the big bad wolf; *Alice in Wonderland* and the accusatorial Queen; *Hansel and Gretel* and the evil witch. Bringing the suspects from these stories to trial and making them account for their actions enables children to revisit these stories in fresh ways and learn about the legal system at the same time. Many of the teachers from our courses went on to develop and hold mock trials with their own classes. Ultimately, we realized that creating scripts for the trials and providing guidelines for how to hold a mock trial might help teachers use this creative resource more effectively. This book is the result.

This book includes scripts for five storybook mock trials that we have successfully used with elementary students in Grades 2 to 7. This book provides information and guidelines to help teachers prepare and implement the trials in their classrooms. In the first section, we discuss the curriculum connections and examine the many benefits of using this educational strategy with children. We have also included suggestions for how teachers and students can develop their own mock trials using stories of their choosing. In an effort to illustrate the various ways people can resolve conflicts outside of the courts, we've also included a chapter on conflict resolution and restorative justice activities.

We hope that teachers and students will use the resources in this book to hold their own trials and that they will see storybook mock trials as an enjoyable, engaging, and productive way of learning more about law and justice in our society.

Wanda Cassidy and Ruth Yates

Acknowledgments

We would first like to recognize the British Columbia teachers, in training at Simon Fraser University, and in practice throughout the Province, who have participated in, created and used fairy tale mock trials in their classrooms. Both they and their students have inspired the activities that are described here. Heather Gascoigne, Principal at Sir Sandford Fleming Elementary in Vancouver, in particular, was instrumental in creating, developing, and implementing in her classrooms, most of the mock trials presented here. She has been the inspiration for most of the other activities in the book and tireless in her advocacy of student-centred classrooms. Julie Fortin created the humorous version of Hansel and Gretel, and Tannis Calder gave us a whole new way of looking at Dr. Seuss, demonstrating what innovative teachers can do with classic stories. We appreciate the review comments of a number of teachers in Ontario, each of whom piloted at least one of the activities in their classrooms. Their assessments have kept us aware of the special needs of classroom teachers. Barbara Johnston played an extremely important role as she edited the original text. Her close attention to detail and concern for the needs of the teacher implementing the strategies in the classroom has contributed much to the final product. Our thanks to her cannot be captured in this simple acknowledgment. We are grateful to our colleagues at SFU who worked on the manuscript over its many incarnations, especially, Kieran Egan who patiently adapted his brilliant and imaginative educational theories for our specific needs, Meguido and Marah Zola helped us appreciate the legal dimensions of multicultural stories, Dennis Smith who drew the storybook characters, Eileen Mallory and Devi Pabla who input and stored numerous versions of the chapters and trials as they have grown over the years. The original authors of the stories we have used here, as well as the children who have inspired them and us through countless generations, also deserve our praise and thanks.

The picture of Goldilocks on the front cover was produced by a student playing the role of Court Artist for the mock trial of Goldilocks and the Three Bears, conducted as part of Wanda Cassidy's Education 448 course, Law in the Curriculum.

Contents

Section 3: Other Conflict Resolution Activities

Introduction

Just as no one is ever too young to participate in legal debate - "No fair!" "You copied!" "Why can't I?"- no one is ever too young to learn about law and justice – not just about the rules and processes which govern society but also, more broadly, the ideas that are at the foundation of our law, its great impact in our lives, and our daily interaction with it.

Conflict is a part of everyday life, and children are always assigning guilt and responsibility, making and enforcing rules, and questioning and testing the limits of authority. Yet while children have firm notions about what is fair or just, they often do not yet have the communication skills needed to untangle disputes or the analytical skills to understand another person's point of view. The storybook mock trials and conflict resolution activities introduced in this book provide an engaging and safe way for children to develop their understanding of fairness and justice and how these concepts relate to rules and law. Further, the experience of participating in a trial can help children understand more about social responsibility and citizenship.

Storybook mock trials are make-believe trials based on well-known and well-loved stories. Fairytales provide the perfect story form for a trial because they have a simple story structure and because they deal with issues important to children: fairness, justice, good and evil, right and wrong. It's easy and fun for children to participate in the structure of a trial and concentrate on larger issues when the story is a simple but captivating fairytale. For example, everyone knows the story of the three little pigs, but what if we shift perspective and give the poor wolf a fair trial? Perhaps, as Sneezy the Wolf argues in our script, he was suffering from hay fever and accidentally blew down the pigs' houses when he stopped by to welcome them to the neighborhood. Similarly, what would happen if Hansel and Gretel were charged with murder of a helpless old woman and stealing her jewels for their own personal gain? No longer seen as the victims, Hansel and Gretel must defend their actions. This shift in perspective has children look at these classic stories in a new light.

By holding a simulation of a real trial and putting these well-known characters on the stand, children not only learn about law and justice but also discover how to identify with a role, how to articulate a perspective, and how to give a reasoned decision. Through this experience, they enhance their ability to appreciate different points of view, weigh the reliability of evidence, and reflect upon issues of power and social responsibility.

The mock trial also provides an ideal cooperative learning experience. For the event to succeed, students need to work together in small groups, then in larger groups, and finally with the full class for the trial itself. Each student plays a different but important role, and each role fits into the larger scheme, like the pieces of a jigsaw.

As we know, the learning experience is far more powerful when children are emotionally and intellectually engaged. The mock trial provides a framework for students to grapple firsthand with important legal, moral, and ethical issues. The students actually become defense lawyers or prosecution lawyers and have to articulate their line of reasoning, or they become witnesses or members of the jury and have to provide evidence or make a decision about guilt or innocence. As a result, the students have to engage with the evidence and sift through differing perspectives.

In doing so, they experience the depth and richness of learning that comes from being immersed in another world.

Structure of the Book

The book is divided into four sections:

• Section 1 provides the theoretical foundation for mock trials and examines why storybook mock trials provide such a valuable learning experience for children. Chapter 1 illustrates how storybook mock trials and conflict resolution activities fit with prescribed learning outcomes and in chapter 2, education professor Kieran Egan examines why fairytales and other fantasy stories so effectively help children learn about reality.

• Section 2 contains information on how to go about planning and implementing a scripted mock trial with children. Step-by-step guidelines are included on how to plan and conduct a mock trial, from warm-up role play activities that open the students to the imaginative process to post-trial discussion questions to help children reflect on the experience and outcomes of the trial.

• Section 3 introduces a number of related activities for upper elementary students. Chapters are included on how students can design and conduct their own criminal trial or civil mock trial based on a story or an event of their choosing, and a chapter that focuses on alternative activities, such as negotiation, mediation, and justice circles that can be used to resolve conflicts in a less adversarial fashion and also bring people together. Also included is an annotated list of story ideas that work well for mock trials and other conflict resolution activities.

• Section 4 includes five mock trial scripts based on fantasy stories, which teachers will wish to photocopy for students use: Goldilocks and the Three Bears, Alice in Wonderland, The Three Little Pigs, Peter Pan, and Hansel and Gretel.

Fairytales and children's stories provide many opportunities to help children explore legal issues, restore justice, and learn ways to resolve conflicts. The mock trials and conflict resolution activities presented here provide a vehicle for examining these issues and concepts in a highly interactive and productive fashion. This resource will also support teachers' efforts to address the important curricular issues of literacy and social responsibility.

Section 1: Why Do A Storybook Mock Trial?

This section focuses on the theoretical issues underlying the value of storybook mock trials as learning experiences for children. Chapter 1 looks at how mock trials meet curricular goals and examines the educational and pedagogical issues involved with teaching using storybook mock trials and conflict resolution activities. In chapter 2, education professor Kieran Egan, examines the role fairytales and other fantasy stories play in helping children learn about reality.

Chapter 1: The Place of Mock Trials in the Curriculum

The use of mock trials and conflict resolution activities in the classroom introduces children to practical experience in problem solving and decision making. By identifying with a character and taking part in analyzing and resolving dilemmas that others face, children learn to become more empathetic, better critical thinkers, and more socially responsible.

Children intuitively understand that someone should listen with an open mind when they have a complaint, that they should be treated fairly, that there are consequences when they have hurt someone else or someone has hurt them. Children expect adults to make fair and reasonable decisions when dealing with such complaints. Their expectations of adults are similar to the expectations adults have of the legal system, which is one of the tools society uses to solve problems that individuals cannot fix themselves. Both adults and children should realize that it is always better to try to solve problems without resorting to the legal system, and that going to court should be the option of last resort. It is important that children learn the skills that will enable them to analyze and resolve their problems successfully and to make good decisions. Mock trials and other conflict resolution activities are designed to teach these particular skills.

Meeting Curricular Goals with Mock Trials

Many fundamental curricular goals can be addressed through students' participation in a mock trial. The mock trial and other conflict resolution activities are particularly suited to the language arts and social studies curricula. The following outcomes have been extracted from various provincial curriculum guides.

Language Arts

•Read, listen, and speak to:
  • explore thoughts ideas, feelings and experiences
  • respond personally and critically to oral, print, and other media
  • manage ideas and information
  • enhance clarity and artistry of communication
  • respect, support, and collaborate with others
  • develop questions
  • clarify meaning
  • think critically
  • build understanding
• Develop openness to new ideas
• Apply effective communication skills

- Read widely and experience a variety of children's literature
- Make language choices to enhance meaning and imaginative writing
- Identify, summarize, express, and respond to information, ideas, perspectives and opinions
- Make judgments and draw conclusions on the basis of evidence

Social Studies

- Engage in active inquiry and critical and creative thinking
- Engage in problem-solving and conflict resolution with an awareness of the ethical consequences of decision-making
- Conduct research using varied methods
- Organize, interpret, and present findings, defend opinions
- Communicate ideas and information in an informed, organized, and persuasive manner
- Demonstrate social compassion, fairness, and justice
- Recognize roles, rights, and responsibilities in school and community
- Acquire the skills, knowledge, and values necessary to understand Canada
- Demonstrate a commitment to democratic ideals and principles, including respect for human rights, principles of social justice, equity, freedom, dissent, and differences and willingness to take action for the public good
- Critically analyze and research social issues
- Solve problems and address conflicts in creative, ethical and non-violent ways
- Demonstrate an awareness of the needs, rights and feelings of others
- Compare personal thoughts and beliefs with those of others
- Be aware of civic and social rights and responsibilities
- Demonstrate an understanding of the Canadian justice system
- Understand the purpose and function of laws
- Relate fiction to real life experiences
- Develop communication skills
- Recognize career opportunities
- Practice social citizenship skills

Assessing Learning

Mock trials and conflict resolution activities address literacy and social responsibility objectives in a powerful way, and they provide a rich source of evaluation data for teachers. Through every step of the process, learning outcomes can be observed, documented, and tested. There are many opportunities for teachers to observe children working independently, cooperating in small groups, and participating in large group discussions and activities. The group process can also involve self-evaluation and peer assessment. Students can submit journals describing their contributions and reflections. Students can then be assessed not only according to how well they meet the expectations of their role but also with regard to their increased understanding of court processes, principles of justice, and the role of different court personnel. In the chart following, some ideas are outlined for academic and social learning.

Instructional Strategies	Learning Outcomes	Assessment
Story Development 1. Reading/listening to a story 2. Analysis of plot and characters 3. Awareness of purpose and perspective	Listen attentively and demonstrate an awareness of the needs, rights, and feelings of others Compare thoughts and beliefs to those of others Experience a variety of children's literature	Recall plot and characters in a story Identify relevant evidence Identify issues in conflict Suggest alternative outcomes
Warm-Up Activities 1. Role play feelings 2. Oral description of visual observations 3. Talk through differences 4. Defend a position 5. Take opposite positions	Cooperative learning Role taking Resolving problems Discussion participation Articulating feelings	Participate in group activity Communicate effectively Prepare reasoned arguments See a different point of view
Background Information 1. Laws and their enforcement 2. Purpose and function of the courts 3. Procedure in a trial 4. Roles of court personnel	Make community connections Discover their place within broader social community Acquire background knowledge of the legal system Understand the role of law in regulating society Practice critical thinking Separate fact from fiction	List significant laws Identify the role of the courts Follow trial procedure Identify court personnel
Mock Trial Preparation 1. Group and collaborative work 2. Strategy planning 3. Evidence gathering 4. Role taking 5. Research implementation 6. Developing questions 7. Presentation preparation 8. Event planning 9. Facilities management	Co-operative learning Search for supporting facts Simulate real life experiences Express creativity Develop sense of social responsibility Replicate citizen involvement Build empathy through participation Find a just solution to conflict	Contribute to group effort Accept a role Prepare role - memorize part Develop an opening statement Prepare questions and appropriate responses Make presentation - follow script Organize for trial Set up classroom/courtroom
Mock Trial 1. Follow court procedure 2. Oral presentation 3. Fulfill responsibilities 4. Role play 5. Analyze evidence 6. Summarize information 7. Make a decision based on evidence	Follow instructions Speak in public Collaborate effectively Assume and sustain a role Support a position with evidence Clarify and summarize information Make a judgment based on evidence	Follow through on group plans Prepared for presentations Articulate responses Organized evidence Oral and written summaries Propose viable decision
Post Trial Activities 1. Debriefing 2. Analysis of experience 3. Awareness of perspective 4. Assessment of process	Empathize with others Summarize what has been learned Appreciate other perspectives Build self-esteem Analyze experiences	Express personal opinion Reflect on experience Motivated to change attitudes and behaviors

For each stage of the mock trial, the instructional strategies are outlined and these are connected to learning outcomes and various assessment opportunities.

Engaging Children in Learning

Mock trials and other conflict resolution activities engage children's emotions and promote their social development. These activities provide opportunities for children to identify with different roles, such as the accused, a witness, a lawyer, or a jury member, and to understand different points of view. In a mock trial, students also experience the process of determining relevant facts to support a case, weighing evidence, and assessing arguments; these tasks help children refine their problem-solving kills. Students are also drawn into an analysis of important value questions such as: What is the impact of hurtful behavior? Who is responsible? What is a fair punishment? How is the problem best resolved? How can we all become more socially responsible?

It is sometimes difficult for children to recognize their own mistakes or faulty decision making. By engaging in role play, children are able to work through the mistakes of others and analyze in open and non-threatening ways why certain characters did what they did. Children can also see different and creative ways to resolve the dilemmas posed by the story. Lessons from the fantasy world then can be applied to the real world. Through role play, children also experience how the justice system works and are able to grapple firsthand with important legal and democratic principles such as fairness, impartiality, due process, the right to be heard, the importance of evidence, and the notion that someone is innocent until proven guilty.

There is evidence in the educational literature to show a strong relationship between emotional engagement in learning and attitudinal change. If students experience for themselves the challenge of balancing interests so that adversaries can appreciate each other's position, there is more likelihood of changing attitudes (Damon, 1977 and Manley-Casimir, Cassidy, and LeBaron, 1993). The presentation of differing perspectives and the search for an equitable solution lies at the heart of the mock trial and other conflict resolution activities.

Research also suggests that children learn better from activities which are investigative, hands-on, and provocative (Joyce and Weil, 1996). Engaging children in the process of resolving a problem is more instructive than simply telling them about ways it might be done. Preparing for a mock trial and acting out the various roles provides children with an innovative framework for working through complex relationships.

Studies in pedagogy also suggest that assuming a role enables children to differentiate the perspectives of self and others. This experience enhances their ability to understand another's capabilities, personality attributes, expectations, desires, feelings, motives, potential reactions, and social judgments (Joyce and Weil, 1996). Role play is a form of social cognition intermediate between logical and moral thought. Because it permits children to feel, act and think like characters in stories, role play helps children relate to situations, empathize with story characters, and understand more fully the concepts and topics presented in a story.

Role play is also a valuable tool for enhancing the emotional and moral functioning in children. When children are encouraged to act on sound moral values based on a sense of human dignity, justice, fairness, and equality, they are developing and exercising good citizenship skills. As students simulate scenarios where these values are tested they begin to more fully understand the values presented. Experiential learning can assist students to think independently and collaboratively and thereby become more responsible and participatory citizens (Solomon, 1987).

Of course, a mock trial based on fairytale characters and events is also enjoyable. Children can imagine fantasy characters tangling with danger, threats, and other scary things. They are motivated to untangle the predicaments in which the storybook characters find themselves. Imaginative activities increase children's language learning because they can use contextual clues to derive the meaning of words, sentences, and paragraphs. Notions of self and self-worth are enhanced by experiences that involve the original, imaginative, and spontaneous interpretation of a character. The chance to play that role in a cooperative setting with other students in a group also strengthens the child's sense of identity and value (Carlton, and Moore, 1966). Others claim that "creative dramatics or role playing develops the whole child without diminishing the uniqueness of the individual, allowing each child to make a contribution in a risk-free atmosphere" (Miller and Mason, 1983, p. 128). Role play gets children on their feet, relieving boredom and allowing for a fresh start on learning tasks. Role-play activities allows children to make decisions about problems which are real to them, allows them to take responsibility for decision making, asks them to be responsible, and lets them interact with each other so that they are exposed to different points of view and reasoning processes.

The mock trial is also an excellent cooperative learning activity. Each child has a role that fits into the overall scheme of the simulation, like the pieces of a puzzle. If one piece is missing, or if one student fails to do his/her task, the whole puzzle is incomplete. However, because the trial includes many different kinds of roles, all requiring differing skills and abilities, each child can find a role in which he or she excels. A more verbally articulate student might play the lawyer, a student with a flare for dramatics might choose to be a witness, a creative student might choose to be the court artist, and a quieter student might play the sheriff or court reporter. This differentiated model allows every student to succeed individually as well as within the larger group.

References

Carlton, L and R.H. Moore. (1966). "The effects of self-directive dramatization on reading achievement and self-concept of culturally disadvantaged children." *The Reading Teacher, 20*, 125-130.

Damon, W. (1977). *The social world of the child*. San Francisco: Jossey-Bass.

Joyce, Bruce and Marsha Weil. (1996) (5th ed.). *Models of teaching*. Boston: Allyn and Bacon.

Manley-Casimir, M., W. Cassidy, and M. LeBaron, (1993). The educational value of mock trials as an instructional approach at the elementary school level." (unpublished paper). Burnaby, BC: Centre for Education, Law and Society, Simon Fraser University.

Miller, G.M. and G.E. Mason, (1983). "Dramatic improvisation: Risk-free role playing for improving reading performance." *The Reading Teacher, 37* (2), 128-131.

Solomon, W. (1987). "Improving students' thinking skills through elementary social studies instruction." *Elementary School Journal, 87* (5), 557-569.

Chapter 2: Reality, Fantasy, and Mock Trials

Kieran Egan

When children participate in mock trials, there is no doubt they are quickly engaged in the experience. Children can become intensely involved in these trials, and many claim afterward that they thoroughly enjoyed themselves. But are they learning any realistic knowledge and skills? Is a mock trial nothing more than an acted-out fantasy story? This dilemma can become pointed for teachers when they switch the focus of a mock trial from such fantasy characters as the Three Little Pigs, Goldilocks, or Alice in Wonderland to realistic topics close to home, such as who egged the teacher's car or who stole money from the school secretary's desk. Trials based on fairytales and other fantasy stories are usually engaging and even exciting for children, while more realistic ones commonly fall flat.

This difference in experience can be puzzling to many teachers; their own educational studies have often emphasized that children are concrete thinkers who will be most readily engaged by, and find most meaningful, realistic material closely connected with their own everyday environments. If the fantasy materials are much more successful in making the activity work, are the children simply engaged by these familiar stories and their characters but not engaged by the law? Are they actually learning anything realistic? Does the fantasy element in mock trials suggest that entertainment has displaced education?

I believe that the fantasy content that seems so important to the success of mock trials does not detract from their educational value. Children's engagement with the fantasy material does not mean that they are cut off from dealing with reality. Indeed, it is the fantasy content that helps the child to grasp the real issues in a meaningful and tangible way.

The Importance of Context

We value fairytales and fantasy stories so highly because they put us into a context that tells us securely how to feel. For example, by itself, the event "the bear went into the forest" tells us very little. For one thing, we do not know what to feel about it. Is it good or bad, dangerous, or wonderful, that the bear went into the forest? If we learn that the bear was trying to escape from some hunters who wanted its skin, we might feel glad that the bear managed to escape into the forest. On the other hand, if we discover that hunters are lying in wait in the forest to catch the bear, then our emotional response to the event "the bear went into the forest" might rather be pity or fear. Unless, of course, we then learn that the bear has cruelly eaten some children and their father, and the hunters want its skin to warm the destitute widow and her surviving baby through the coming winter.

These examples might not be the makings of a classic story, but the point is that we don't know how to feel about "the bear went into the forest" until we have reached the end of the story, when we know the total context of the events. Indeed, we know we have reached the end of a story when we know how to feel about all the events that make it up. That is why computers can't recognize stories as distinct from other kinds of narratives. Stories are those kinds of narrative that help us frame emotional responses to the elements that make them up. No other form of language, no other narrative, tells us so clearly "how" to feel about the events and elements presented.

The problem with life and with history is that we can never know securely how to feel about them. As new things happen, we continually have to reassess how we feel about past events. Egging a car or stealing money exist in an affective vacuum. Like "the bear went into the forest," the events of vandalism or theft remain unclear without the context of a story. But we do know how to feel about Goldilocks or about Hansel and Gretel because they exist in the context of an emotion-orienting story.

As adults we commonly separate out for analytic purposes our perception of events, our feelings about them, and our thinking about them. However, in real life we do not perform these three tasks separately; we perceive, feel, and think at the same time. The incessant focus in education on rational thinking has tended to hide the fact that we hardly ever simply "think" about anything without involving our feelings. This fact is perhaps even truer for children, who have not been schooled so long toward purely rational thinking. Their emotions are commonly tied up with thinking.

Consequently, fairytales present children with a particularly welcome environment for understanding thoughts, perceptions, and feelings. A mock trial of Goldilocks for the theft of Baby Bear's food takes place in the context of a story in which the children's emotions are already involved. This emotional – and imaginative – grasp on the content of the trial is far from a trivial matter. Without it, children are missing one of the most important tools they have for making sense of an experience. With it, one of the most important tools children have for making sense of experience is being actively deployed.

The emotions evoked by classic fairytales and other fantasy stories include courage and cowardice, security and fear, hope and disappointment, cleverness and stupidity, energy and sloth, and so on. The stories raise the most profound conflicts we experience in life. While the mock trials take place in what seems like a playful setting, the playfulness supplies the protective context within which to address these profound issues. Bruno Bettelheim has discussed in detail the important role the classic fantasy tales can play in the healthy psychological development of children. He compares their role with that of myths in traditional oral cultures. As he writes, "myths and fairy stories both answer the eternal questions: What is the world really like? How am I to live my life in it? How can I be truly myself? The answers given by myth are definite, while the fairy tale is suggestive" (1976, p. 45). The degree of children's engagement in the stories, and in the mock trials built on them, should indicate that something more important than trivial entertainment is going on.

Arthur Applebee, who has studied children's understanding of stories extensively, elaborates on how classic fantasy tales deal with reality under the surface level, as it were:

> The stories [children] hear help them to acquire expectations about what the world is like – its vocabulary and syntax as well as its people and places – without the distracting pressure of separating the real from the make-believe. And although they will eventually learn that some of this world is only fiction, it is specific characters and specific events which will be rejected; the recurrent patterns of values, the stable expectations about the roles and relationships which are

part of their culture, will remain. It is these underlying patterns, not the witches and giants which give them their concrete form, which makes stories an important agent of socialization, one of many modes through which the young are taught the values and standards of their elders. (1978, pp. 52-53)

The mock trial that uses fantasy story material is nevertheless demonstrating and establishing patterns of expectations and values that help children grasp important features of reality. I think we need not fear that these fantasy-based mock trials are dealing only with trivial and frothy content as far as the children are concerned.

In addition, the mock trial itself takes the form of a story. It has a beginning in which the conflict it established, a middle in which the conflict is elaborated and complicated, and an end in which the conflict is resolved. That is, the important qualities of any story apply doubly to mock trials. Mock trials rely on the context of a well-known story, and they work out a story within that overall context.

Fantasy and the Everyday World

Why are children so readily engaged by fantasy characters, such as talking rabbits, pigs, or bears? If learning does proceed from the local and immediate and gradually expands outward – that "constant expansion of horizons" John Dewey insistently argued for (1916/1966, p. 175) – then children's fascination with fantasy creatures and unbelievable situations is puzzling. It is inadequate to say that these are the kinds of creatures that are presented to children in stories. The audience plays a major role in determining the kind of story presented to it. If children responded equally enthusiastically to realistic tales, then their storybooks would not be full of talking animals.

Consider how children build up their conceptions of most of the phenomena of their everyday world. We see them constantly forming oppositions like hot/cold, soft/hard, big/little, wet/dry, and so on. Bettelheim suggests this procedure is necessary because children first need to establish frames of reference or contexts in order to come to grips with reality. "Since polarization dominates the child's mind, it also dominates fairy tales," he argues (1976, p.9). These polarizing oppositions provide the most general frames of reference for children's exploration of reality. Think, for example, about how a child begins to develop some conceptual grasp over the temperature continuum. At the beginning, the child necessarily understands only the concepts of "hot" and "cold." "Hot" simply means "hotter than my body's temperature," and "cold" means "colder than my body's temperature." Later, the child will mediate between these two concepts and develop the concept of "warm." As C.K. Ogden states: "When once an opposition is established and its principle understood, then either opposite, or any intermediate term, can be at once defined by opposition or degree" (1967, p. 20).

What has this theoretical point to do with the three little pigs and mock trials? The environment of the child is made up not only of a continuum between the big and the little, the hot and the cold, the soft and the hard, and so on. The child's world is also made up of discrete, discontinuous things like human and animal, nature and culture, life and death. What happens when you try to make sense of oppositions like human and animal using the procedure that helps you develop a conceptual grasp over the material world? First, you develop concepts that distinguish between people and animals, but then you try to mediate between the oppositions. And what do you get when you mediate between human and animal? Among much else, you get the three little pigs. They are animals, but, they are dressed in clothes, they can talk, they want to build safe homes for themselves, and so on.

When a mock trial draws on the story of the three little pigs rather than on three children in the neighborhood, it is tying into that area of intellectual activity most energetically engaged in developing a conceptual grasp over reality. The three little pigs might seem the antithesis of reality, but two realistic things seem to be going on in such fantasy tales. First, the content being dealt with concerns life and death, fear and anxiety, safety and danger, love and hate, and a range of the most powerful emotional material we face as human beings. That children face these emotional challenges within the confines of fantasy stories provides them with insulation against the implications these challenges may have in reality. But one cannot argue that the stories are driven by the most basic emotions and values we humans experience.

The second fact is that the procedure of forming oppositions and mediating between them seems responsible for generating fantasy worlds. Fantasy stories engage children so vividly not because they are removed from reality but because coming to terms with the unreality of the mediating categories is of crucial importance to children as they develop clear conceptions about the range and limits of reality.

Set within the context of an overarching story, each mock trial is based on stark oppositions. The structure of any trial sets up the opposition in the beginning, then elaborates on it. In a mock trial the elaboration involves asserting the opposing positions and trying to make one of the two opposing viewpoints persuasive and the other doubtful. The child engaged in the mock trial is examining the events from one perspective and then the other, and the child is probably finding both positions persuasive at one time or another. Even though the ending of the trial (particularly a criminal trial) has to assert the victory of one position, that convention does not obliterate the different perspectives the child has experienced. While the end is not a mediation – a "warm" from "hot" and "cold," as it were – in the child's mind the simplicity of the beginning will already have been through quite complex mediation. One discovery children will commonly make is that, even in the stories that form the basis of mock trials, the truth is rarely as simple as it might at first seem.

It is worth remembering, also, that the contents of children's fantasy tales are, in significant degree, similar to the contents of the myth stories of the world. Of particular interest here are those half-animal, half-human creatures that are ubiquitous in myths. We know that myths are not some intellectual frothy confection waiting only for rationality to come along and make them redundant. Rather, myths involve subtle intellectual strategies for making sense of the world and experience. While full of what we may consider fantasy content, myths deal very adequately with the real world of their users. Not dissimilarly, children's engagement with fantasy is not some obvious intellectual defect to be cured immediately but is rather one of the strategies humans use to come to terms with reality.

The Abstract Foundations of Fantasy

As suggested above, if we consider the kinds of emotional categories that underlie most children's fantasy stories, we find such abstract concepts such as love and hate, anxiety and security, good and bad, courage and cowardice, and so on. In other words, whether the story involves Hansel and Gretel, the three little pigs, Peter Pan, or another fictitious character, dramatic conflict between opposite emotions lie just under the surface of the story. It is as though the story itself exists to articulate and resolve the underlying conflict, which is based on these essential abstractions of life.

Through these abstractions, the concrete content is made meaningful and engaging. The mock trials based on fantasy tales are engaging because underlying the tales, and so underlying the trials, lie the most powerful abstract ideas we ever deal with. Children grasp the surface content of the trials by wrestling with the emotional abstractions beneath them. While it is generally supposed that children easily understand the concrete aspects of their daily lives, the fact is that they access these "realities" through their consideration of the abstractions.

Mock trials have significant educational merit. Not only can children learn the basic elements of legal principles and democratic behavior, but at the same time they also have the opportunity to consider more subtle issues that are at the heart of educational development for their age. The engagement we commonly see when children participate in mock trials is not simply an acting out of a fantasy; it demonstrates in a profound sense an involvement with reality and with issues of deep human significance.

Unlike reality stories, the use of fairytales and fantasies is crucial to the educational success of mock trials and essential to helping focus children's minds on the content and procedures of the trial.

Moreover, setting the mock trials in the context of fairytales ensures that the emotional orienting power of the story form can help make the content meaningful. The fantasy content does not remove the mock trial from the real world; rather, it provides the means for young children to address important features of reality. The fantasy surface does not prevent realistic learning, and the abstract concepts that figure so prominently in fairytale mock trials give children access to the concrete content that forms the explicit material of the trials. Mock trials are indeed of significant educational value, in part due to the fairytales and fantasy stories on which they are based.

References

Applebee, A.N. (1978). *The child's concept of story.* Chicago: University of Chicago Press.

Bettelheim, B. (1976). *The uses of enchantment.* New York: Knopf.

Dewey, J. (1916/1966). *Democracy and education.* New York: Free Press.

Egan, K. (1988). *Primary understanding: Education in early childhood.* New York: Routledge.

Hayek, F.A. (1970). "The primacy of the abstract." In A. Koestler and J.R. Smythies (eds.), *Beyond reductionism.* New York: Macmillan, p. 309-323.

Ogden, C.K. (1976). *Opposition.* Bloomington: Indiana University Press.

Section 2. Guide to the Storybook Mock Trials

There is a vast range of ways to stage a mock trial. Mock trials can be held in a classroom, in the school gym, or in a courtroom or other public setting borrowed for the occasion. Participants can wear elaborate costumes or they can wear a simple sign indicating who they are. It can be staged for the whole school with friends and families invited, or it can involve only the members of the class. Regardless of how a mock trial is staged, there are numerous learning opportunities, and students will have a lot of fun as they prepare for the trial. This section is a companion to the five mock trial scripts and includes information on what students and teachers need to do to stage a mock trial. The storybook mock trials are suitable for Grades 2 to 7, and we've recommended grade levels for each script, as follows:

Goldilocks and the Three Bears: Grades 2 to 3

Three Little Pigs: Grades 3 to 5

Peter Pan: Grades 3 to 5

Alice in Wonderland: Grades 4 to 7

Hansel and Gretel: Grades 5 to 7

The pre-trial activities, group-work preparation, and post-trial activities for the scripted mock trials can be modified to fit any of the elementary school grades.

Chapter 3 provides the following step-by-step directions for getting started.

• Timeline
• Including families
• Warm up activities
• Essential legal information for teachers

Chapter 4 describes how to organize the trial itself.

• Identifying roles and tasks
•Casting
•Planning logistics

Chapter 5 outlines the steps involved in holding the actual trial, and chapter 6 deals with important post-trial activities such as discussion and debriefing sessions.

Chapter 3: Getting Started

As the class starts to prepare for the mock trial, some preliminary activities help familiarize everyone with the kind of work involved and the tasks to come. This chapter includes information about timelines, the importance of involving families in the mock trial preparation, and some ideas for warm-up activities, which can help introduce students to the nature of role-playing and the importance of drawing on their imaginations. This chapter also provides some basic principles of the law, so teachers can introduce the concept of the law to students and explain specific issues as necessary, along with an overview of the storybook mock trial scripts.

Timeline

The actual staging of a trial can take up to two hours. The amount of time a class spends on preparation before the trial depends on how elaborate the trial is. In general, organizing and staging a mock trial takes about 10 hours of class time. To keep up the momentum and to build group cooperation, it is better to organize the mock trial as an intensive experience where students work on it an hour or so every day for two to three weeks, rather than as an intermittent activity that students turn to once a week over several months. Students can do much of their preparation at home, such as making their costumes, and learning their lines.

It is also important to allocate class time after the trial for debriefing and extension activities to allow students to get out of role, reflect on their experiences, and extend their learning into related areas. Post-trial debriefing and activities can take up to two hours.

Here is a rough guideline of how to organize the time:

Week 1: warm-up role play activities, introducing the idea of law, reading the story organizing groups and role selection.

Week 2: group work, learning parts, preparing props and costumes

Week 3: staging the trial, post-trial discussion and post-trial extension activities

Involving Families

Mock trials are a great way to involve parents in the process of their child's learning. Teachers are encouraged to send a letter home explaining what the class is doing, and the educational benefits of the mock trial. Invite parents to participate. You may find parents who work in an area of the law, and who might act as the judge or a consultant for the mock trial. Parents can also play an important role by helping their children learn their parts and make their costumes. Parents may also want to be involved if the trial is held in the local courthouse or public place. By watching the event, parents can see evidence of their children's learning and experience firsthand the satisfaction students feel from successfully demonstrating their new skills and knowledge.

Warm-up Role Play Activities

Participating in a mock trial gives students the chance to take on a new role and play a character entirely different than themselves. Students will vary as to the ease with which they can take on different roles, so warm-up exercises are important for those who feel inhibited in some way. These warm-up activities will help students become more comfortable with taking on a new role for the trial and help them appreciate the difference between reality and imagination.

Persuasion

Students work in pairs. Each partner chooses a color and has three minutes to convince their partner of why their color is the best. Partners can use any means of verbal persuasion.

Mirrors/Shadows

Working in pairs, one student initiates the movement and the other student is the mirror and tries to copy the movement. The student who is initiating the movement begins by moving slowly. Both keep eye contact. The exercise is working when the two begin to move as one. Emphasize that cooperation is the aim, not trying to confuse the "mirror." This activity allows students to practise cooperating and concentrating.

Point of View and Role Reversal

Put students in two lines sitting on chairs facing one another, knee to knee. One side argues the affirmative with the person in front of them. The other line argues the negative. Give each side a couple of minutes to argue their case. Then each person on one side moves over one chair and makes the argument with the next person. This continues for a two more moves. The students then switch sides and argue the other position. It's best to use silly ideas, such as blue is a better color than green; cats make better pets than dogs; winter is the best time of year. When the activity is over, give students a chance to debrief; they can discuss what the two roles felt like and whether they gained any new perspectives or found new solutions. This activity gives students experience in persuasion and point of view.

Role Play from a Photograph

In small groups, students look through a newspaper or magazine to a find a photo that appeals to the group. The group members develop a scenario based on what they think is happening in the photograph. Each student then takes on the role of someone in the photo. Using the photo as a guide, students bring it to life by role playing the situation.

Experts

Students work in small groups so that each student has a chance to become an expert in a particular field. Encourage students to be creative when they think up possible "experts," such as an expert on wrinkle cream for rhinoceroses, or a wizard who's an expert on magic spells. The others interview the "experts" to test them on their knowledge of the field and their ability to answer questions. Interviewers could assume the role of television reporters. Working in role, students should try to convince the others of their expertise by answering the questions as authentically as possible.

Making Quick Decisions

Students work in pairs or small groups to solve a conflict. They are given roles or an outline of a situation. In role, they are given a problem or conflict to solve, in which they only have just a couple of minutes to come up with a solution. At the end of the allotted time, students share their solutions with the entire class. Students share how they reached a decision and how they felt under the pressure of time.

A Basic Introduction to Law and Legal Procedures (for teachers)

A teacher does not have to be a lawyer or an expert in law to put on a mock trial. You need to know something about the law and legal procedure before undertaking a mock trial with students. You may also be able to use this information as a handout for older students. A glossary of key legal terms is included in Appendix A. More information on law resources, including legal education organizations and websites, is included in Appendix B.

Courts

A court trial is often called a hearing because a judge (or a judge and jury) hears the matter before making a decision. Courts deal with criminal matters where the state (represented by the police, government, and prosecutors) charges an individual for an offence. Courts also hear civil or private matters. When two individuals or groups cannot come to an agreement, they may decide to take their problem to court. Civil law covers all laws that aren't criminal. (See chapter 8 for more information on civil court trials). All of the scripted storybook trials in this resource deal with criminal matters.

Criminal Court

A crime has been committed when a person breaks one of the laws set out in the Criminal Code of Canada. If a person commits a crime, such as stealing, breaking into somebody's house, or murder, the police lay a charge, and the state follows up on this charge by bringing the accused to court. The state or society brings the accused to court because certain offences are considered a crime against all of us – they contravene our fundamental values and beliefs as a nation. The state is represented by Crown counsel, which is the prosecution. In this book, we use the terms "prosecutor," or "prosecution team," rather than "Crown."

If the prosecution team thinks they have a good case against the accused, they will set up a trial date and prepare a case. The prosecutor is responsible for proving that the accused is guilty beyond a reasonable doubt. The accused usually acquires a lawyer and together they work together to provide the best defense against the accusation.

Because all the powers of the state can be used to prosecute a case against an accused, many safeguards have been established to protect the defendant's rights. The legal rights set out in sections 7 - 15 of the *Canadian Charter of Rights and Freedoms* are designed to ensure that the state does not abuse its powers. This means that when the police think a crime has been committed there must be reasonable grounds before they can search or seize a suspect. Accused individuals must be informed of the charges against them; they must be able to contact a lawyer and they must be tried within a reasonable time. It is also the accused's right to be presumed innocent until guilt is proven in a fair hearing.

Before the trial, the prosecution lawyers and the defense lawyers do a lot of work to prepare. They investigate the crime, gather evidence, examine witnesses, write appropriate questions for witnesses, study the relevant law, and prepare their arguments. The prosecution is responsible for proving the case against the accused, so prosecution lawyers must be very thorough in the way they prepare their evidence and witnesses. The prosecution should also present a clear picture of the crime and the series of events that led up to the crime. The defense counsel only has to show that there is reasonable doubt that a crime was committed or that the person accused committed the crime, so preparation of the defense depends on how much evidence the prosecution has against the accused. The prosecution has a duty to show the defense counsel what evidence it has so that the defense can prepare its own case adequately.

Court Procedure

The way a court hearing is conducted (often called court procedure) differs according to the kind and level of court that is hearing the matter. All of the scripted storybook trials follow the procedure used in a Canadian Provincial Superior (or Supreme) Court. This is the court that usually hears serious matters such as crimes where the punishment is more than two years imprisonment and civil cases where the damages would be more than $10 000. Depending on the severity of the crime, a person may have the option to have the case heard by a judge alone or by a judge and jury. If a judge alone hears the case, the judge decides whether the accused is guilty or not guilty based on the evidence. The judge then decides on the punishment from a range of sentences set out in the Criminal Code of Canada. A jury is a requirement for the most serious crimes. When a jury is involved, the jury decides whether the accused is guilty or not guilty and the judge determines the appropriate sentence.

Legal Terminology

Following are some key terms that are used throughout this discussion of a mock trial, which the teacher may need to explain to the students. These terms are also included in the glossary in Appendix A.

Trial: A hearing before a judge, or a judge and jury, to decide if a law has been broken.

Verdict: A finding by the court that a person is guilty or not guilty.

Evidence: The information presented by the lawyers and witnesses during a trial.

Exhibit: An object, such as a fingerprint chart, a piece of cloth, or a letter, which is used as evidence by lawyers to prove a case.

Sentence: The punishment that a judge orders after an accused person is found guilty (such as imprisonment or fine).

Discussion of the Idea of Law and Justice

Children often associate the law only with the police, criminals, and jails. Many don't realize that the law touches all aspects of our lives and that police officers and jails are only part of the legal system. Before starting work on the mock trial, it's helpful to assess students' understanding of the law, courts and justice system. Below are some simple activities and discussion questions which may be used to assess pre-knowledge before introducing the role and function of the various participants and the purposes of a trial.

Ideas for Activities

These activities help students think about how the law affects them and can lead to a broader discussion about the law and trials.

Have students review a newspaper and circle all items related to law.

Ask students to examine a TV guide and circle all shows related to law, the police, and the courts.

Show a videotape of a television news broadcast and then ask students to identify all stories related to law.

Have students record everything they did that morning from the time they woke up until they arrived at school, and then discuss how each of these activities is influenced by law.

Ideas for Discussion

Below are a few ideas for provoking discussion about the law, courts, and trials. These questions can lead to other questions and help students think about the role of courts and the meaning of justice in our society.

Brainstorm the words that come to mind when you hear the word "law."

Brainstorm the words that come to mind when you hear the word "court."

Is a law different than a rule?

What is the role of lawyers in a court?

Why do we have prosecution lawyers as well as defense lawyers?

Why are crimes considered to be against all of us in society?

Why are crimes prosecuted by the state?

Is it important that an accused obtain a lawyer? Why?

What does a judge do?

Why do we have juries? What is the jury's role?

What does "innocent until proven guilty" mean?

During this discussion, some of the students may mention law shows on television. Explain that most of these shows are made in the United States, which has a different legal system than Canada.

Reading the Story

Most students will probably be familiar with the stories on which the scripted mock trials are based. However, since there is sometimes more than one version of the storyline, the teacher may want to read the story again to the students or have them read it themselves so they're reminded of the plot, characters, setting, mood, theme, and problem or conflict in the story. Once the students have read the story, the teacher can review the facts, characters, and issues and work with the class to identify the dilemmas. These dilemmas can then be related to law and the criminal mock trial, so students see the connections.

About the Storybook Mock Trials

The following are brief summaries of the five stories and the criminal charges on which each trial is based.

Goldilocks and the Three Bears

Recommended for Grades 2 to 3

While three bears – Papa Bear, Mama Bear, and Little Baby Bear – take a pleasant walk a young girl named Goldilocks comes across their house in the forest and decides to enter. The bears return from their outing to find that someone has been tasting their porridge, sitting on their chairs, and sleeping in their beds. To Baby Bear's dismay, he discovers that someone has eaten his porridge and broken his chair. In fact, the intruder, Goldilocks, is still there sound asleep in Baby Bear's bed. Upon hearing the Bears' voices, Goldilocks wakes up and runs from the house, badly frightened.

In this mock trial, Goldilocks stands charged that she

• Did commit a theft of a value not exceeding $5 000 by willfully stealing porridge, the property of the three Bears, contrary to section 334(b) of the Criminal Code of Canada.

• Did commit mischief by willfully damaging a chair belonging to Baby Bear, contrary to section 430(1) of the Criminal Code of Canada.

Goldilocks pleads not guilty to both charges.

The Three Little Pigs

Recommended for Grades 3 to 5

Three porcine siblings set off to build their houses. The first little pig, who builds with straw, and the second little pig, who builds with twigs, fall victim to a hungry wolf who huffs and puffs and blows their houses down. Both pigs run from their dilapidated shelters to seek refuge with their brother. The third little pig, who builds his house of solid brick, has better luck. The wolf is unable to blow down his solid brick house, and the third little pig outwits the wolf by tricking him into climbing down his chimney and landing in a pot of boiling water.

The mock trial assumes that all the little pigs survive the wolf's attacks and that the wolf, after being captured by the third little pig, is arrested and put on trial.

In this mock trial, Sneezy the Wolf stands charged that he

• Did commit mischief by willfully damaging the first little pig's house of straw, contrary to section 430(1) of the Criminal Code of Canada.

• Did commit mischief by willfully damaging the second little pig's house of twigs, contrary to section 430(1) of the Criminal Code of Canada.

• Did commit mischief by willfully attempting to damage the third little pig's house of brick, contrary to section 430(1) of the Criminal Code of Canada.

• Did commit break and enter of the third little pig's house of brick, with intent to commit an indictable offence therein, contrary to section 348(1)(a) of the Criminal Code of Canada.

Sneezy the Wolf pleads not guilty to all charges.

Peter Pan by J.M. Barrie

Recommended for Grades 3 to 5

Peter Pan is the story of the boy who would not grow up. One night, while listening to bedtime stories outside the Darling home, Peter and his loyal fairy companion Tinker Bell fly into the nursery of the Darling children – Wendy, John, and Michael. The three children decide to follow Peter Pan and fly with him to Neverland, a magical place free of grown-up rules. Here they experience wonderful adventures and meet mermaids, hang out with the Lost Boys, and encounter the evil Captain Hook and his crew of pirates, who have an ongoing battle with Peter Pan.

In this mock trial, Peter Pan stands charged that he

• Did unlawfully take Wendy, John, and Michael Darling to Neverland, with the intent to deprive Mr. and Mrs. Darling, the parents, and Nana, the family's nurse dog, of them, contrary to section 281 of the Criminal Code of Canada.

Peter Pan pleads not guilty to this charge.

Alice in Wonderland by Lewis Carroll

Recommended for Grades 4 to 7

A girl named Alice sees a white hare hurrying down a rabbit hole. She follows him down the hole and finds herself in Wonderland, a place where she meets an eccentric cast of characters and discovers that she can shrink to miniature proportions or grow to the size of a giant if she samples the wrong drink or food. On her fantastic adventures in Wonderland, the Mad Hatter, the Cheshire cat, and the weeping Mock Turtle are just some of the unconventional characters Alice meets. On one of her adventures, Alice wanders into the royal tea of the diabolical Queen of Hearts and, quite unintentionally, creates havoc. "Off with her head," demands the Queen as Alice narrowly escapes the Queen's guards.

In this mock trial, Alice stands charged that she

• Did cause a disturbance in or near a public place, namely the Queen of Hearts' garden, by fighting and shouting, contrary to section 175(1)(a) of the Criminal Code of Canada.

• Did steal a box of currant cookies, the property of the White Rabbit, of a value not exceeding $5 000, contrary to section 334(b) of the Criminal Code of Canada.

Alice pleads not guilty to both charges.

Hansel and Gretel

Recommended for Grades 5 to 7

Two children, Hansel and Gretel, are abandoned in the forest by their cruel stepmother and loving but weak-willed father. The children come across an enchanting house made of gingerbread, cake, and candy. As the children nibble on the house, they realize they are eating the home of an old woman, who entices the children inside, locks Hansel in a cage, and forces Gretel to work for her. The two siblings foil the witch's plan to fatten them up and eat them when Gretel gets the key from the witch, releases Hansel, and pushes the witch into the oven. The children are reunited with their loving father and live happily after.

In this mock trial, Hansel and Gretel stand charged that they

• Did commit mischief by willfully damaging private property belonging to the witch, contrary to section 430 of the *Criminal Code of Canada.*

• Did commit break and enter of the witch's residence, with intent to commit an indictable offence, contrary to section 348(1)(a) of the Criminal Code of Canada.

• Did commit a murder of the witch, contrary to section 229 of the Criminal Code of Canada.

• Did commit theft over $5 000 of pearls and precious stones belonging to the witch, contrary to section 334(a) of the Criminal Code of Canada.

Hansel and Gretel plead not guilty to all charges.

Chapter 4: Preparing for the Mock Trial

The next step is to prepare for the mock trial. This includes choosing students for the roles, helping students as they learn their roles and prepare their costumes, finding an adult to play the judge, and selecting a location for the trial. Each of these tasks is discussed in this chapter.

Choosing Students for the Roles

When students have a basic understanding of the law and have read the story, it's time to introduce them to the various players in the criminal courtroom and to discuss the expectations of each role. Because the choice of students is critical to the success of the trial, teachers may want to assign students to the various roles or hold auditions. A description of the key roles is included here, along with a summary that can be handed out to the students.

The **prosecution** and **defense lawyers** have significant roles in the mock trial so students with strong verbal and analytical skills are well suited to these roles. Because the lawyers have such significant roles, there are three lawyers for the prosecution and three lawyers for the defense in each mock trial script. The lawyers for the prosecution and the defense should be somewhat balanced in terms of verbal and organizational skills.

The **accused** and the **witnesses** are also significant roles and best played by students who like to dress up, have a dramatic flair, and can use their imaginations to bring the role to life. To prepare for these roles, students should think about how their character would talk and move; they should try to "become" their character.

The **court clerk** role is important for keeping everything on track. The court clerk reads the indictment, swears in the witnesses, labels the exhibits, and assists the judge. The court clerk is best played by a student who is organized and has a loud and clear speaking voice.

The **court reporter, sheriffs,** and **jury** have limited speaking lines but have important responsibilities before, during, and after the trial. These roles may suit students who don't like the spotlight. The court artist and media roles might appeal to students who are artistic, like to write, or have a flare for technology.

Keep in mind that there is always flexibility with the number of roles. If the class is large, the jury or media contingent can be larger, or additional court artists or photographers can be added. If the class is smaller, the numbers of students in certain roles may be reduced accordingly. There is also a lot of flexibility with the jury. While there are usually 12 jury members in a real trial, a mock trial can have any even number of jurors. Another option is to ask another class, or parents and friends to act as jurors in the trial. The inclusion of "outsiders" can add a dimension of excitement and suspense to the trial, as these people come in fresh, not knowing the nature of the story or the issues involved. In this way, they are more like the jurors picked in real life from a voters list.

Choosing the Judge

Because the judge plays the pivotal role in keeping the trial on track, responding to issues that surface during the trial, and keeping the trial moving, this role is best played by an adult. It is helpful, but not necessary, to have someone who has some courtroom experience. Perhaps a judge, police officer, lawyer, or a law student could play the role. Or perhaps a parent with some legal background would participate. Another option is to ask the school principal, the district superintendent, or another teacher. Ideally, the classroom teacher should not be the judge. The teacher's role is to facilitate the trial and see that it is implemented smoothly. As well, the event can take on an aura of authenticity and excitement if the judge is someone relatively unknown to the students.

Who's Who in the Criminal Courtroom

Judge: The pivotal court official who manages the court. The judge listens to evidence, instructs the jury on their role, hears the jury's verdict, and sentences the accused if guilty. In a trial with no jury, the judge decides if a person is guilty or not guilty.

Prosecution: A lawyer who represents the Crown (the government) and who presents information to try to prove that a crime has been committed and that an accused person has broken a criminal law.

Defense Counsel: A lawyer who presents information to show that either a crime was not committed or the accused person is not guilty of breaking a criminal law.

Accused: The person the prosecution claims has broken a criminal law.

Witness: A person who gives information during the trial.

Jury: A group of people that find a person guilty or not guilty of breaking the law. They must all agree on the verdict.

Court Clerk: The person who assists the judge in the courtroom by swearing in witnesses and supervising the exhibits during the trial.

Sheriff: The person who maintains security in the court, protects the judge and watches over the accused.

Preparing for the Trial

Once the students have been assigned their roles, divide the class into the following three groups:

Group 1: Prosecution Team

Prosecution lawyers (3 students)

Witnesses for the prosecution

Group 2: Defense Team

Defense lawyers (3 students)

Witnesses for the defense

Group 3: Court Personnel, Jury and Media Team

Sheriff, court clerk, and court reporter, court artist, newspaper journalist, television reporter, and members of the jury

Each group should be kept busy preparing for their part in the trial. One of the keys to a cooperative learning exercise is that all students are occupied in productive and engaging ways. The teacher will likely find that each group monitors its own members, which ensures that each student contributes. The teacher's role during the group process is to spend some time with each group making sure they are on track and occasionally bringing together the full class as common issues arise.

The courts must follow very strict rules of procedure so that everyone feels they are being treated fairly when they appear before the court. While the mock trial can be more flexible, students must still learn their roles well and understand what is expected of them. Note also that students do not have to follow the questions exactly as written in the scripted trial. Although they should stick to the story line, they should also be encouraged to improvise. During the trial only the lawyers will be allowed to refer to the script. Witnesses should not bring the script to the witness box.

If members of the class are the jury, it's best to keep the jury quite small in numbers. There is not a lot of preparation for the jury before the trial so it is important that these students take an active role in making costumes, providing props for the story, and learning about the juror's role and responsibilities.

While members of the media research the role of the media prior to the trial, prepare a short news report, and assume their role during the trial, their greatest responsibilities are after the trial. When the trial is over, they should be expected to interview the witnesses and lawyers, write articles, and put together a short newspaper article. The media is also responsible for showing the videotape after the trial, along with a commentary on the event. Older children may also edit the recording of the trial into a newscast. Court artists should be responsible for mounting an exhibition of the trial drawings in the classroom or hallway.

Information Sheets and Role Cards

Role cards help students understand what is expected of them as they work with their group and during the mock trial. Sample role cards are provided in the following pages. These can be used as blackline masters or photocopied for handouts to each team.

Group 1: Prosecution Team

The prosecution team consists of three lawyers for the prosecution and usually three prosecution witnesses. This group will have a lot of preparation work to do before the trial. Depending on the age of the students, they may be encouraged to develop their own questions and use the script as a guideline only.

To prepare for the trial, prosecution lawyers will

- Decide who will be prosecution lawyer 1, 2, and 3 and divide the responsibilities of each lawyer according to the tasks needed.
- Become well acquainted with the script by practising questions for the defense witnesses and cross-examination questions for the prosecution.
- Consider developing one or two new questions for each witness, which could develop the prosecution's argument further. (This is optional depending on the age of the students.)
- Discuss in their group what other questions the defense team might ask, and how the prosecution witnesses can be prepared for these questions.
- Practise the opening statement and closing arguments.

To prepare for the trial, prosecution witnesses will

- Prepare their responses to the questions. It is better if they understand their role and answer in their own words as opposed to memorizing the script word for word.
- Work with prosecutors to prepare for possible new questions the defense team might ask.
- Think about how to portray their character. They should rehearse how their character would talk and move and try to "become" their character.
- Create their costume.

Group 2: Defense Team

The defense team consists of three defense lawyers and usually three defense witnesses. This group will have a lot of preparation work to do before the trial. Depending on the age of the students, they may be encouraged to develop their own questions and use the script as a guideline only.

To prepare for the trial, defense lawyers will

- Decide who will be defense lawyer 1, 2, and 3 and divide the responsibilities of each lawyer according to the tasks needed.
- Become well acquainted with the script by practicing questions for the defense witnesses and cross-examination questions for the prosecution.
- Consider developing one or two new questions for each witness, which could develop the defense team's argument further. (This is optional depending on the age of the students.)
- Discuss in their group what other questions the prosecution might ask, and how the defense witnesses can be prepared for these questions.
- Practise the opening statement and closing arguments.

To prepare for the trial, defense witnesses will

- Prepare their responses to the questions. It is better if they understand their role and answer in their own words as opposed to memorizing the script word for word.
- Work with the defense team to prepare for possible new questions the prosecutors might ask.
- Think about how to portray their character. They should rehearse how their character would talk and move and try to "become" their character.
- Create their costume.

Group 3: Court Personnel and Media

As this is the most diverse group, it's best to appoint someone in the group to act as group coordinator. Not all roles described below are necessary, but if there are a lot of students in this group, it works well to divide this group into smaller subgroups during the planning process and have the subgroups meet as a whole group from time to time.

Officers of the Court

Officers of the court (court clerk, court reporter, and sheriffs) are expected to help with trial preparation to ensure the trial runs smoothly. To prepare for the trial, court personnel will

- Review the trial procedure at the beginning of the script to learn how the trial should proceed.

- Study the court diagram to figure out how to set up the classroom or gymnasium for the trial (or, if possible, book a courtroom).

- Do some research in the library and on the Internet to find more about their roles in the court (see Appendix B for suggestions on organizations and websites).

- Gather or make all the exhibits to be presented by the prosecution and defense during the trial.

- Arrange to have a video or audio tape recorder (for the court reporter) available on the day of the trial.

- Prepare costumes.

- Keep a journal of their own activities, as well as questions or ideas that have come up during their preparation for the trial.

The Media

To prepare for the mock trial, members of the media will:

- Decide who plays the roles of newspaper journalist, television reporter, the photographer, and court artist. (There can be more than one of each.)

- Research what makes a good news story by examining newspaper articles, watching news reports, and, if possible, talking to journalists.

- Interview witnesses and/or lawyers before the trial, take still pictures, and make sketches.

- Prepare a short news report prior to the trial including information from preliminary interviews along with sketches and photographs. Circulate the report to other members of the class, including the teacher.

- Arrange to borrow a video camera so the television reporter can record the trial. Note: In a real trial no cameras (video or still) are allowed in the courtroom; however, in a mock trial videotapes and still pictures are important to the learning process. If the class holds the mock trial in a real court house, it is important to get permission before using any recording devices.

- Prepare their costumes.

The Jury

To prepare for the trial, the jury will

• Decide on who will be foreperson of the jury. The foreperson is the spokesperson for the jury and will tell the judge what the jury's decision is.

• Discuss the process of making a decision.

• Develop a costume that reflects the setting in which the story being tried takes place. See the section following on costumes for more information; the scripts also include specific costume suggestions.

• Find or make the necessary props for the trial exhibits.

• Research the role of the jury at the school library and on the Internet.

• Write a report on why they voted that the accused was innocent or guilty. Ask them to explain how the jury system works, what influenced their decision in the mock trial, and what they found challenging about separating fact from opinion.

Prosecution Team Role Card

The prosecution (also called the Crown counsel) is the team that works for the government and presents information to try to prove that a crime has been committed and that an accused person has broken a criminal law.

Here are the things you must do.

1. Read the story or the script
2. Describe the accused
3. Decide what information you need to get from the witnesses.
4. Divide up the tasks for your team

• Prepare an opening statement for the trial
• Divide up the witness list between the members of your team and practice the questions that each of you will ask in court.
• Prepare for questions the judge might ask during the trial
• Prepare a closing statement

Witnesses Role Card

The witnesses are characters in the story who give information during the trial and tell the court what they know about the facts of the case. A witness may be someone who saw the crime happen, someone who can offer important information that relates to the case, or an expert in a field that brings new information to the case (such as a fingerprint expert). Both the prosecution and the defense are allowed to call witnesses to help their cases.

Here are the things you must do.

1. Read the story or script and learn about your character

2. Make a costume and find props to help you act like the character

3. Prepare the answers to questions the lawyers may ask you

4. Remember you must tell the truth according to the story when you testify in court

Defense Team Role Card

The defense counsel is the team of lawyers who presents information to show that the accused person is not guilty of breaking a criminal law. The defense team tries to show that the prosecution has not proven its case. They do this by finding flaws in the prosecution's evidence or legal reasoning.

Here are the things you must do.

1. Read the story or the script

2. Describe the accused and each of the witnesses

3. Decide what information you need to get from the witnesses.

4. Divide up the tasks for your team
    • Prepare an opening statement for the trial
    • Divide up the witness list between the members of your team and practice the questions that each of you will ask in court.
    • Prepare for questions the judge might ask during the trial
    • Prepare a closing statement

Officers of the Court Role Cards

Court Clerk Role Card

The court clerk is the judge's assistant who helps the judge run the trial in an orderly way.

Here are the things you must do during the trial.

1. Announce the opening and closing of the court
2. Read the charge against the accused
3. Swear in each witness and ask them to state their name for the court
4. Label and look after exhibits
5. Follow the script during the trial.

Sheriff Role Card

The sheriff is person who maintains security in the courtroom, protecting the judge and the accused.

Here are the things you must do during the trial.

1. Review the script and make or find a costume
2. Assist with setting up the courtroom
3. Escort the accused into the court and sit nearby during the trial

Court Reporter Role Card

As the court reporter, you are responsible for:

1. Recording the trial and writing down the times that witnesses begin and end their testimony.
2. Arrange for a tape recorder.
3. Write down important things that each witness says.

Media Role Card

The media report the progress of the trial to classmates, the school, and parents. Members of the media include newspaper and television journalists and court artists. You sit in a designated area in the courtroom to take notes and make observations during the trial. Most of your work, however, will come before and after the trial.

Before the Trial

1. Find out what makes a good news story by reading a real newspaper, watching television show.

2. Identify the following parts of a news story: who, what, when, where, why, and how.

3. Take photographs of the groups preparing for the trial.

4. Keep notes of the progress of the trial preparation.

5. Prepare a poster advertising the trial for your school and a letter for parents.

During the Trial

Videotape the trial
Take notes
Draw picutres of the courtroom, and participants

After the Trial

- Prepare qustions to ask when you interview the witnesses and lawyers. For example, you may ask them:
- What was your role in the trial?
- Do you think the accused got a fair hearing?
- What do you think of the decision?
- Are you satisfied with the judgment
- What impact has this crime had on your life?

Write a newspaper article of videotape a report of the trial for the media.

Jury Role Card

The jury in a real court case is made up of 12 ordinary citizens, picked from the voters list whose job is to listen to the testimony and then determine whether a person is guilty or not guilty of breaking the law. They must assume the accused is innocent until he/she is proven guilty.

This is what you will need to do:

1. Read the story,

2. Assist with the preparation of the courtroom and costumes for the other characters

3. Decide on the foreperson who tells the judge the jury's decision

4. During the trial, listen carefully to the testimonies and keep notes about what you have heard

5. When it is time for the jury to deliberate,

• the first step is to ask each juror whether they think the accused is guilty and explain why or why not.

• If everyone does not agree at first, you must try to come to an agreement.

• After each member of the jury has had a chance to speak, everyone votes on whether the defendant is guilty or not guilty.

• The majority determines the verdict

Judge's Role Card (for adult)

The judge is the court official who works alone or with a jury to decide if an accused is guilty or not guilty of breaking the law. The judge explains to the members of the jury what their job is, hears the case, and presides over the courtroom. The judge is impartial, meaning he/she does not side with either party and therefore can make a fair decision. If the jury finds the accused guilty, the judge is responsible for deciding the sentence (punishment), such as a fine or imprisonment.

As the judge is in charge of the courtroom and the trial, it is your responsibility to ensure the trial is conducted fairly and properly. You will be able to have the script with you while you judge the case, but you should also review the script so you know how the trial will proceed. Because students are encouraged to add their own questions and not follow the script exactly, some of the questions and responses may be different than what is written in the script. The judge is also welcome to add comments and ask questions that are not in the script.

You will also want a copy of the court procedure with you in the trial. Before the trial, review what it means to it means to "sustain" or "overrule" an objection. Learn about what is meant by "guilty beyond a reasonable doubt," "leading questions," "hearsay evidence," and "badgering the witness." The teacher can provide a glossary of these terms.

Once all the witnesses have been called and the prosecution and defense lawyers have made their closing statements to the jury, the judge instructs the jury on the laws that are involved in the case. The judge then outlines to the jury the various options that are open to them – to either find the defendant guilty or not guilty for each of the charges – and to allow the jury 15 minutes to deliberate.

Sentencing

Although the judge may want to look at the options provided in the Criminal Code of Canada, it can be fun to provide some lightheartedness to the fairytale cases and make the sentence fit the fairytale crime. For example, on one occasion when a mock trial was held of Goldilocks, the judge asked Baby Bear to name his favorite food. Baby Bear replied that it was chocolate brownies (and not porridge). The judge sentenced Goldilocks to a year's probation and community service, which involved baking brownies each week and delivering them to Baby Bear, as well as staying out of trouble. Another creative sentence might be to require the wolf in The Three Little Pigs to take a course in carpentry and rebuild the homes of the first and second little pigs. The judge has the right to choose an innovative response if the accused is found guilty on any charge.

Preparing Costumes

Costumes add a sense of drama and excitement to the mock trial. All of the scripts have costume suggestions for each of the characters but students can use their imaginations in coming up with appropriate costumes. Perhaps some parents could help prepare costumes or help with face painting on the day of the trial. It may be possible to borrow robes for the lawyers, court clerk, and court reporter. If this isn't possible students can make robes with black construction paper.

To participate more actively in the trial preparation, members of the jury should also prepare costumes. For example, jury members for Alice in Wonderland could dress up as a deck of cards by preparing large sandwich boards that fit over their heads. Jurors participating in the Goldilocks trial could be various animals in the forest, and jurors for the trial of Hansel and Gretel could be trees in the forest.

Selecting a Location for the Trial

It may be possible to stage the trial in an actual courthouse or other public venue. Contact the local courthouse to see what is possible. If the mock trial is being held in the courthouse, or school gymnasium, parents, friends, and fellow students could be invited, as this enhances the learning process and adds an element of excitement to the whole process. If the trial is to be held in the classroom, then rearranging tables and chairs can transform the classroom into a courtroom. Plan to have the jury deliberate in their courtroom seats, so that everyone can watch that process.

A diagram of a typical criminal courtroom is included on the following page.

People in a Criminal Trial

The drawing below illustrates a typical criminal courtroom. You may wish to set up your classroom in a similar way.

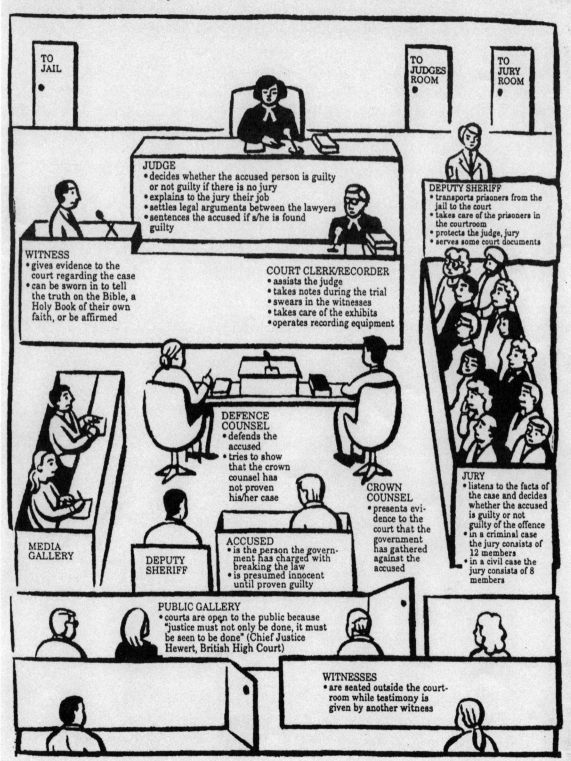

Used with permisssion of Law Courts Education Society of British Columbia

Chapter 5: Staging the Storybook Mock Trial

This chapter includes information on standard court procedures and how to ensure the trial runs smoothly. You should allow approximately 2 hours for the entire trial, including 5 to 10 minutes to get everyone seated and introduce the trial, about 50 to 60 minutes to stage the trial, 10 to 15 minutes for jury deliberations, and 10 to 15 minutes for post-trial discussion. On the day of the trial, it helps to have everyone enter the courtroom in an orderly fashion. If the trial is taking place in a courthouse or school gym with a large audience, students can seat audience members in the public gallery. When the audience is seated and everyone is ready to begin the trial, the teacher should welcome the guests and review the intent of the trial. (See the suggested script which follows). The prosecution and defense teams should then enter and sit at their tables. Next the media and witnesses enter and sit in their designated areas. The sheriff then enters with the accused. The accused sits in the prisoner's box with the sheriff close by. The court clerk and court reporter then arrive and take their places.

Once the trial is over, it is very important to the learning process to hold a de-briefing discussion, so that students can come back to "reality" and share some of their thoughts about the experience.

Introducing the Trial

The teacher should introduce the trial if it is being "performed" before a group of fellow students, parents, and guests. You would begin by welcoming participants and guests involved in the trial, outlining the intent and format of the mock trial.

Today you will see (name of the accused) standing trial on criminal charges of _____. There are three important elements of a criminal trial that you should keep in mind:

1. The accused is innocent until proven guilty.

2. The onus is upon the prosecution to establish guilt.

3. In order for the accused to be found guilty, guilt must be established beyond a reasonable doubt.

The accused is here today after having been arrested, made an initial appearance in court, had bail set, and promised to appear for this trial.

We must point out that liberty has been taken with today's trial procedures. Thus, you will observe a few things not ordinarily done in a real trial. For example, the accused person charged with these type of offences normally would be tried in lower provincial court with a provincial court judge, whereas we are holding the trial in the Supreme Court with a jury. And if the person being tried is under age 18, he/she would be dealt with by the Youth or Family Court, not the

Supreme Court (which is for adults). Witnesses do not normally hear other witnesses' testimony, as they will today. The jury usually deliberates in private. In this court the jury will come to its decision in our presence, jurors usually must come to a unanimous decision, whereas in this trial we recognize a majority decision.

Trial Procedure

Court Clerk stands and says "Order in the Court. All rise." The judge and jury enter and the trial proceeds as follows.

1. The court clerk reads out the indictment.

2. The prosecution and defense lawyers introduce themselves to the judge, stating what they intend to prove and listing witnesses who will be called to testify.

3. Prosecution makes an opening statement stating what they intend to prove and naming their witnesses.

4. Prosecution calls the first witness to the stand.

5. Defense cross-examines the first witness.

6. Prosecution calls the second witness to the stand.

7. Defense cross-examines the second witness.

8. Prosecution calls the third witness to the stand.

9. Defense cross-examines the third witness.

10. Prosecution rises and says to the judge that the prosecution's case is concluded.

11. Defense makes a short opening statement to the jury, outlining their defense and listing their witnesses.

12. Defense calls the accused or first witness to the stand.

13. Prosecution cross-examines the accused or first witness.

14. Defense calls the second witness to the stand.

15. Prosecution cross-examines the second witness.

16. Defense calls the third witness to the stand.

17. Prosecution cross-examines the third witness.

18. Defense says that the defense case is concluded.

19. Defense makes a closing statement to the judge and jury.

20. Prosecution makes a closing statement to the judge and jury.

21. The judge makes a brief statement to the jury, reviewing the charges and instructs them to decide their verdict.

22. The judge, lawyers and the accused leave the courtroom and the jury conducts its deliberations in their places.

23. The jury discusses the trial and signals to the court clerk when they have reached a verdict.

24. The court clerk says, "Order in the court. All rise."

25. The judge, lawyers and accused enter the courtroom.

26. The judge asks the jury for the verdict.

27. The foreperson reads out the verdict of guilty or not guilty for each charge. If the accused is found guilty of any charge, the judge will impose an appropriate sentence. If the verdict is not guilty, the judge will tell the accused that he/she is free to go.

28. The court clerk adjourns the court.

De-briefing Discussion

The mock trial is over after the judge either sentences the accused (if the verdict is "guilty") or tells the accused he or she is free to go (if the verdict is "not guilty"). However, the opportunities for reflection, discussion, and debate have just begun. It is important to spend about 15 minutes right after the mock trial for the students to debrief the event. This session gives the students a chance to talk about what happened in the trial and to come out of role. The discussion can take place even if an audience is present, and it may enhance the session to ask observers about what they learned in the process of watching the trial. This discussion also sets the stage for further post-trial discussion and activities that may follow.

Below are some examples of the kinds of questions that may be asked. The idea is not to discuss any one issue in depth, but rather to allow students to decompress and share some immediate thoughts about the process they just experienced.

Jurors

• What kinds of issues were raised in your discussion?

• How unanimous were you in your voting?

• What evidence was most persuasive?

• Which characters were more believable?

• Why did you come to the decision you reached?

Lawyers

• How did you feel about your presentation?

• Which arguments did you feel were most persuasive?

• Would you have done anything differently?

• What did you like (or dislike) most about being a lawyer?

Witnesses

• What did it feel like being in the witness box answering questions?

• Did anything surprise you about the trial and the way it unfolded?

• Which part of your testimony were you happiest with?

Officers of the Court

• Why is your role as court clerk/court reporter/sheriff important?

• What role did costumes play in giving the trial believability?

Media

•What would you like to write about or comment on when you produce your newscast?

Judge

• an informed adult, who was not part of the pre-trial preparation, what did you find most interesting about this trial?

• Are you surprised by the jury's decision?

• Why did you choose the sentence you did?

Observers

• What did you learn about the trial?

• Would you have made the same decision if you were the jury?

Once the trial is over, there are still many opportunities for encouraging students to consider the issues raised and for engaging in learning opportunities. Post-trial activities can include discussions, debriefing, visits to courtrooms, writing story sequels, and many other activities, as examined in the next chapter.

Chapter 6: Post-trial Activities

The post-trial discussion and post-trial activities are as important as the trial itself. This is when students reflect on what happened during the mock trial, analyze what they did and how they felt playing a role, and consider the impact that the process had on their character and on other participants. The discussion and activities also allow students to move beyond an understanding of the procedures used in the courts toward an examination of the social dilemmas inherent in an adversarial system; they can also think about the bigger questions surrounding conflict resolution in general. Some post-trial ideas are outlined as follows.

Debriefing

During the mock trial, students may experience strong emotions and attachment to their character. Sometimes it is difficult for students if they were on the side that "lost" the case. Because the courts follow an adversarial system, the accused is either found guilty or not guilty. It is not possible to be somewhat guilty. Students need to see that the most important issue is that the accused had a fair trial and that both sides clearly argued their case. This is an important principle of law, and this cannot be reduced to winners and losers. During the post-trial period, students need to talk about the characters they portrayed, the surprises they encountered, and the emotions they experienced.

Sometimes the teacher needs to mediate between the role player and the simulation much as a director does in a motion picture or a stage drama. The director knows what the actor needs to draw from the script in order to build a credible portrayal of the character. Similarly, the teacher must lead his/her students to understand that the purpose of the mock trial is to understand what another person is thinking and feeling and to appreciate the difficulty of experiencing a conflict where someone has suffered a loss and another person is responsible and must be held accountable. It is important to help students understand what bias means and how crucial it is for courtroom personnel to be neutral. Participants in a trial must be able to make sound and reasonable arguments, discover truth based on evidence, and not make unsupported judgments.

These realizations about law and justice often do not come during the course of the simulation but afterward, in retrospect. Learning is reinforced when good discussion questions are asked while the memory of the activity is fresh in the minds of the students. The following questions will help achieve these learning goals.

Discussion Questions on the Judicial Process

• Does the court process give everyone involved a fair chance to state their case?

• Do you think you were given a fair chance to present your side of the story?

• Was the accused treated fairly?

• What other information did you need before you could come to an appropriate decision?

- Why does the court discourage witnesses from expressing their opinion?

- Did the jury (or judge) come to the right decision in the case? Why or why not? Do you feel that the punishment fit the crime? Why or why not?

- Were you satisfied with the results of the trial? Why or why not?

Discussion Questions on Personal Involvement

- How did you feel when you were playing your part?

- Were you able to put yourself in the shoes of your character?

- Did you change your mind about your character over the course of the trial?

- Did you change your opinion of the participants in the trial (the accused, the victim, the judge, the jury) as the event proceeded?

- Did you agree with the decision of the judge/jury?

- What would you have changed in the way you played your role?

- Will you think differently about the law when you read another story about a character accused of committing a crime?

Beyond the Trial: Discussion Questions on Social Responsibility

To take full advantage of the learning opportunity, it is important to move the discussion to the broader issues about law and justice that a mock trial raises. The following questions can help generate discussion about the law, social responsibility, and restoring justice.

- Are there other ways that the characters might have solved their problems rather than going to court?

- Do you think the court solution solved the problem?

- If you were in a similar situation to the main characters, what would you have done?

- Are there better ways to solve problems other than going to court?

- Can you explain the phrase "the punishment should fit the crime?"

- In this case, was the punishment appropriate for the crime?

- An offender should also be rehabilitated, so that he or she does not do the same thing again. Can you suggest some actions that could help rehabilitate the offender?

- How might the relationship between the victim(s) and offender be restored?

- How can individuals get involved in changing a law they don't agree with?

- What have you learned about trial procedures that you didn't know before?

- What questions do you still have about the courts, the legal system, and justice?

- Has your experience in a mock trial changed the way you treat people? How?

- What have you learned about working with a group of people to try to solve a problem?

Students may also discover that taking a matter to court is a complicated and difficult process; they may suggest that it would be better for the parties to avoid the situation in the first place by learning about the law and making a decision not to break the law. A major principle of law is that we don't do anything that will hurt another person or damage their property. A personal decision always to respect the rights of others is an important step toward becoming a responsible citizen. Courts are designed to solve the most serious problems that people find themselves in, but every day we all experience potential conflicts in our lives that we should be prepared to resolve ourselves. How can knowing what the courts do help us to solve our own problems?

Self-assessment

One way of helping students think about these questions is to have them complete a self-assessment questionnaire. Sample student self-assessment forms are included on the next three pages.

Student Self-assessment: Group Participation

Name _____ Date:_____

1. What did you enjoy most about preparing for the mock trial?

2. What did you find most challenging?

3. How successfully did you cooperate with other group members?

4. How might your group have worked more efficiently?

5. Was there a leader in your group? Explain.

6. What did you do if you didn't agree with someone else's idea?

7. What could your group have done differently to prepare for the trial?

8. What would you like to say about working in groups?

Student Self-assessment: The Mock Trial Experience

Name: _____ Date: _____

1. What role did you play in the trial?

2. What were you expected to do in your role?

3. How well do you think you did in your role to contribute to the trial?

4. Is there anything you would liked to have done differently in the trial?

5. How do you feel about the outcome of the trial? Why?

6. What have you learned about courts, trials, and justice as a
   result of participating in the mock trial?

7. What questions do you still have about courts, trials and justice that
   you would like to find answers to?

8. What have you learned about yourself as a result of participating
   in this trial?

Quick Student Self-assessment

Name: _____ Date: _____

Please circle the number that best fits your answer to the following questions:

1. I worked hard to prepare for my role: always   sometimes   never

2. I understood what was expected of me in my role: always   sometimes   never

3. I contributed ideas to my group: always   sometimes   never

4. I listened to other group members   always   sometimes   never

5. I asked for help when I needed it: always   sometimes   never

6. I helped other students in my group: always   sometimes   never

7. I did what I was supposed to do in the trial: always   sometimes   never

On a scale of 1 to 5, (1 being "a little" and 5 being "a lot"), how would you evaluate your experience in preparing for the trial?

1. I enjoyed preparing for my role in this trial:

a lot   5   4   3   2   1   a little

2. I learned from this experience:

a lot   5   4   3   2   1   a little

3. Group members helped me in my role:

a lot   5   4   3   2   1   a little

4. I understood my role:

very well   5   4   3   2   1   not at all

5. I liked doing this mock trial:

a lot   5   4   3   2   1   a little

Extension Activities

After the mock trial the class might engage in a number of activities to extend the learning value of the experience.

Review Recordings of the Trial

If a videotape was prepared of the trial or the jury deliberations, students can watch or listen and discuss the event again. Students usually enjoy seeing themselves on video. Reviewing the recording also provides an opportunity to talk about the legal process, the characterization, and the persuasiveness of the arguments. Reviewing the recording of the jury deliberations also gives students the opportunity to hear the jury's thoughts and to learn what influenced each jury member's decision.

Visit a Courthouse or Police Station

Classes could visit a court to observe an actual trial in progress. The courts are open to the public and children who are old enough to understand the need for decorum in the courtroom are welcome to attend a court session. Teachers can contact the court clerk's office in their area to arrange this. Classes may also be able to visit a police station or meet with police in a community context.

Invite Visitors to the Class

Any number of guests in the law-related area could be invited into the classroom to talk about what happens in a trial or discuss procedures associated with arrest and crime investigation. Consider inviting a lawyer, judge, police officer, forensics expert, sheriff, probation officer, parole officer, or community youth worker to talk to the class.

Rewrite the Original Story

Although it may be wishful thinking, it would be a wonderful world if people could avoid conflict altogether and work out their differences. Avoiding legal problems is like preventative medicine; it is often easier than the cure. After completing a mock trial based on a story, students could be assigned to rewrite the original story so that the offence never arises. For example, if Goldilocks had searched out the bears and asked for something to eat and a place to sleep, they likely would have been happy to accommodate her. The story might be less compelling but it would have had a happier ending.

Students could also relate (verbally or in writing) an experience in their own lives that parallels the events of a story. Ask what they have learned from the story and from the resolution proposed in the mock trial to help them deal with their personal situations.

Write a Sequel to the Story

Ask students to imagine how the trial might have affected the lives of the characters and then to write a sequel to the original story.

Write the Story from the Villain's Perspective

Read The True Story of The Three Little Pigs by John Scieszka to the class. Students will enjoy hearing the wolf's arguments to claim his innocence. Ask the students choose a story and rewrite it in the first person from the villain's point of view.

Exploring Key Concepts from the Trial

Students could do follow-up research on issues they touched on in the trial, such as "innocent until proven guilty." Students should recognize that people accused of crimes have certain rights. Police and prosecutors must follow the rules, and judges must apply the law the same way in similar cases. The state is a very powerful force; to be fair to everyone the police and the courts must follow strict rules when they suspect that someone has committed a crime. Everyone is entitled to a fair hearing and an accused has the right to present a defense. It is only when all the rules have been followed that a person can be convicted of a crime and punished for the offence.

Students could study the legal rights section of the *Canadian Charter of Rights and Freedoms* to examine the rights of an accused person in Canada. Every time a judge makes a decision in a Canadian court, he/she writes a report of the case and gives reasons for the decision. Students could find case reports on the Internet and begin to understand how judges apply the law. Juries are important participants in the court process. When students become adults they might be asked to serve on a jury, so it is worthwhile asking them to investigate the process further. Many Canadian Web sites help to explain the judicial process in language that children understand. See Appendix B for a list of Web site addresses.

Pretend to be the Judge

Each student pretends that he/she is the judge in the case just heard or another story, and the student then writes the judgment. Below is an outline of the main parts of a written judgment; students should follow this outline in their writing.

1. Statement of the main problem or issue. The problem might be that Baby Bear's porridge is missing and his chair is broken and the court must decide whether Goldilocks is to blame.

2. Summary of the key facts of the case

3. Summary of the argument by the prosecution.

4. Summary of the argument by the defense.

5. The decision that is reached, including the punishment if the accused is found guilty.

6. The reasons the judge reached that particular decision.

Section 3: Other Conflict Resolution Activities

Section 3 introduces a number of law-related activities for students in grades 5 to 7.

- How to design and conduct a criminal mock trial from scratch (chapter 7)
- How to create a civil mock trial based on a story or an event (chapter 8)
- Other methods for resolving conflicts (chapter 9)
- Annotated list of story ideas that work for mock trials and conflict resolution activities. (chapter 10)

Chapter 7: Creating a Criminal Mock Trial

If the class is studying a story or novel in which one of the characters commits a criminal offence, a mock trial is a perfect opportunity to promote critical thinking about the plot, setting, and actions of the various characters. Having students develop their own criminal mock trial helps them learn how to synthesize information and examine different perspectives on an issue.

Section 2 outlined how to organize a scripted mock trial. The same procedures can be adapted for a non-scripted mock trial. The main difference between using a scripted trial and having students create their own trial is that students will need more guidance and more preparation time to develop their roles.

Choosing a Story or Scenario

There are an unlimited number of possible stories on which to base a criminal mock trial. Fairytales, fables, and many historical and contemporary novels and stories work well. See chapter 10 for an annotated list of storybooks that could form the basis for a mock trial. Movies and historical events can also be used as the basis of a mock trial. The main criteria is that one of the principal characters seems to have done something that constitutes a criminal offence in Canada, such as murder, aggravated assault (an intentional act that causes another serious physical injury), robbery, theft, slander, or treason. When choosing a story, look for

- well-developed characters and plot

- a protagonist and antagonist who are clearly defined opposing characters

- a wrongdoing in which one character injures or harms the other

- evidence that leads to a well-grounded suspicion that one person deliberately harmed another.

Determining the Crime

After choosing the story and identifying the wrongdoing, either examine the Criminal Code of Canada or contact the provincial public legal education organization to determine the charge. The Criminal Code is available at most public libraries or can be viewed on the Web at http://laws.justice.gc.ca/en/C-46/index.html. All provinces and territories have a public legal education organization that could also help. When students are creating their own criminal trial, it is best not to identify more than two charges, as this could result in a trial that is too complex for students to argue adequately.

An Example of a Criminal Mock Trial:

Lemony Snicket's *The Reptile Room*

Recommended for Grades 5 to 7

We have taken an incident from the novel *The Reptile Room (A Series of Unfortunate Events,* Book 2) by Lemony Snicket, to demonstrate how a teacher might develop a case and organize a criminal mock trial from a story.

About the Story

This popular series of books recounts the misadventures of three children – Violet, Klaus, and Sunny Baudelaire – who were orphaned when their parents died in a house fire. The children, who are to inherit their parents' fortune when they turn 18, are sent by their guardian to live with Count Olaf, a distant and, as it turns out, very unpleasant relative. The first book in the Series of Unfortunate Events tells of the terrible experiences the children endure while in the Count's care. When the children realize that the Count only wants access to their money, they run away. Book 2, *The Reptile Room,* opens with the children's guardian sending them to another distant relative, Dr. Montgomery Montgomery (Uncle Monty).

The children are delighted with this new arrangement; their eccentric Uncle Monty loves them and welcomes them into his home. He is a herpetologist, (a scientist who circles the globe looking for snakes to study) and plans to take the children with him on an expedition to Peru. Unfortunately, Uncle Monty hires an assistant to accompany them on the expedition. When the assistant arrives, the children recognize that he is really Count Olaf, who has disguised himself and is impersonating the assistant. The children cannot convince Uncle Monty that the assistant means to harm them, and sure enough there is an unexpected death. Uncle Monty is found dead in his reptile room, apparently of snakebite. The children are immediately suspicious, but it seems they are powerless to escape the clutches of the wicked and determined Count, who plans to dispose of the children in Peru so that he can collect their fortune.

The children prove that their uncle didn't die of an accidental snakebite but was poisoned with snake venom that was injected with a needle. After a series of events, the children finally manage to convince their guardian that Count Olaf is a murderer, and the guardian calls the police. Unfortunately, Count Olaf escapes and the reader is fairly certain that he will reappear in the next book in the series to pursue the children and their money.

There are several places in this story where the teacher could interrupt the narrative and announce that Count Olaf has been captured, arrested, and charged with the murder of Uncle Monty. (In the book, of course, Count Olaf escapes so it would be necessary to stop reading at an appropriate point so that the mock trial can proceed.) The class could then prepare a trial to determine whether Count Olaf is guilty of murder in the first degree.

Preparing for the Trial

- Introduce the idea of a mock trial by referring to the orientation section of chapter 3.

- Identify the offense and the witnesses and determine which side they will testify for.

- Establish working groups and decide on the roles described on black-line master #1.

- Role cards for the prosecution and defense teams are provided on the following pages..

- Find role cards for the court personnel and media team in chapter 4.

• Arrange for a judge to preside at the trial. The judge should be an adult and preferably someone who isn't familiar with the story.

• Provide an outline of trial process and courtroom arrangement – black-line masters are in chapter 6.

As the students work in their groups, there are a number of things the teacher can do to provide support.

• Help students understand the meaning of the charge against the accused by referring them to the Criminal Code.

• Monitor the prosecution and defense teams to be sure the arguments they develop are consistent with the story.

• Remind witnesses to remain consistent with the story and encourage them to prepare their responses to the lawyers' questions in advance.

• Assist students with finding additional information and resources.

Encourage students to keep a record of their team and individual activities to assist you with assessment.

An information sheet follows to help the groups understand their responsibilities. Role cards are also included and can be photocopied for each team.

Debriefing

After the trial is over, remember to conduct a debriefing session to allow students to step out of their roles and talk about what they learned. Specific suggestions for the debriefing process are outlined in chapter 6.

Prosecution Team

Prosecution lawyers (3 students)

Witnesses for the prosecution (witnesses could include the children, Klaus, Violet, and Sunny, Mr. Poe, and the arresting police officer)

Tasks

• The team decides on the charges to be laid against the Count. (If they agree on a charge of first degree murder, they must prove that the murder was planned and deliberate.)

• Lawyers gather evidence to prove the accusation, such as the syringe and a sample of the snake venom.

• Witnesses prepare their testimony.

• Lawyers interview witnesses to establish that there was intent to murder.

• Lawyers prepare questions for their own witnesses and cross-examination questions for defense witnesses.

• Lawyers prepare opening and closing statements.

• Witnesses finish preparing their testimony and make costumes.

Defense Team

Defense lawyers (3 students).

Witnesses for the defense (witnesses could include Count Olaf, Dr. Lucafont, and a forensic expert).

Tasks.

• The team prepares a theory that explains what happened, for example that the snake really did escape and bite the victim.

• Lawyers gather the evidence that the defense needs to argue the case.

• Witnesses prepare their testimony.

• Lawyers interview the accused and prepare witnesses for the defense.

• Lawyers prepare cross-examination questions for prosecution witnesses to cast doubt on their claims and evidence.

• Lawyers prepare opening and closing statements.

• Witnesses finish preparing their testimony and make costumes.

Court Personnel and Media Team

Court clerk; court reporter; sheriff, media, including the court artist, newspaper journalist, and television reporter; and members of the jury

Tasks

• Read relevant sections of the *Criminal Code of Canada.*

• Study the procedures for a criminal trial.

• Decide who will play the court clerk, sheriff, court reporter, jury members, and members of the media.

• Prepare the statement of the criminal charges.

• Arrange for courtroom or prepare space in class or school.

• Gather the evidence from the lawyers or help prepare the evidence.

• Assist with costumes.

• Do pre-trial and post-trial interviews of witnesses, prepare a news report, and organize an audiotape or videotape of the trial.

• The court artist sketches trial participants and exhibits them.

Role Card for the Prosecution Team

As the prosecutors, you represent the government or the state. Your team is trying to prove that first degree murder was committed and that Count Olaf is guilty beyond a reasonable doubt.

Opening Statement

A team member prepares an opening statement that reviews the facts of the case against the accused and outlines the evidence that your team will present to the court to prove your case.

Questioning Witnesses for the Prosecution

• Frame questions that will create a picture of events leading up to the offense

• Avoid leading questions – get the witness to tell the court what he actually saw by starting your questions with words like who, what, when, where, and how.

Questioning the Defense Witnesses (Cross-examination)

The prosecution also has the chance to question the defense's witnesses after the defense counsel has finished questioning them. This is called "cross-examination."

• ask questions that discredit the witness or show weaknesses in the testimony the witness gives.

• listen carefully during the trial and be able to develop additional questions when they become necessary

Closing Statement

Another team member prepares a closing statement that summarizes the arguments made by your side and states why the accused, in your view, is guilty beyond a reasonable doubt.

Role Card for the Defense Team

As the defense counsel, you are the team of lawyers trying to show that Count Olaf is not guilty of murder. If you can create "reasonable doubt" in the mind of the jury then they must find the accused not guilty.

Cross-examining Prosecution Witnesses

As prosecution presents its witnesses a defense lawyer cross-examines by asking them questions that discredit the witness or show weaknesses in his/her testimony.

Opening Statement

A team member prepares an opening statement that reviews the facts of the case and outlines the evidence that your team will present to the court to prove that the accused is not guilty. You want to show that the accused either did not commit the crime or that if he did he had a good reason for doing so (for example, self-defense).

Questioning Witnesses for the Defense

• Order your list of witnesses and decide if you want the accused to testify or not (this is an option in law.).

• Develop questions for each witness that present the story from the perspective of the accused.

• Try to bring everything out that the witness is able to say to prove the case without suggesting to the witness what to say. One way to get the witness to tell his/her story without leading is to start your questions with words like who, what, when, where, and how.

• Remember that witnesses can only talk about what they actually saw. Telling the court what they heard from someone else is called "hearsay" evidence or "second hand" evidence and is not admissible.

• Listen carefully during the trial and be able to develop additional questions when they become necessary

Closing Statements

A member of your legal prepares a closing statement that summarizes what the defense has proven and why the jury should find the accused not guilty of the charges.

Criminal Law vs. Civil Law

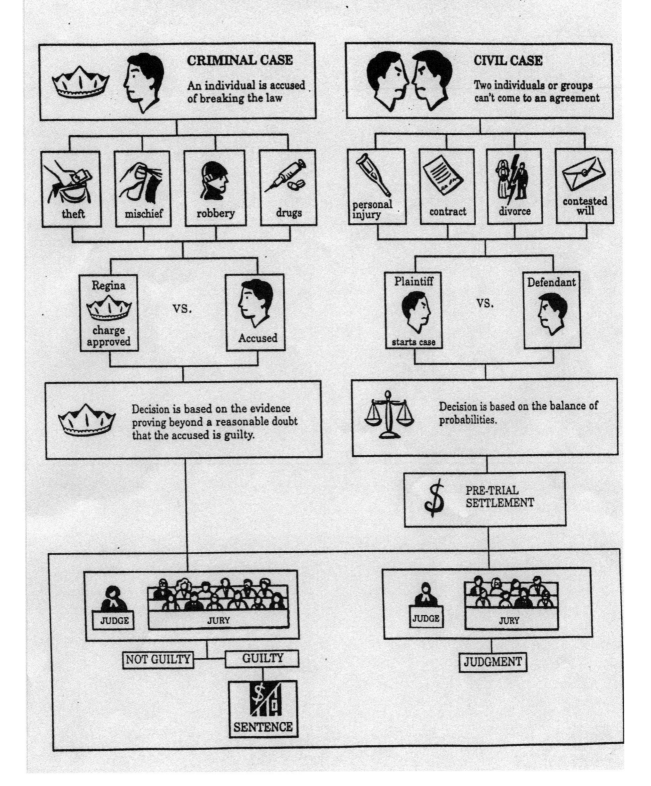

Used with permission of Law Courts Education Society of British Columbia

Chapter 8: Creating a Civil Mock Trial

In a civil case one person sues another for an act that has caused him/her physical, financial, and/or emotional injury. When a person is injured as a result of another person's carelessness, the injured person can sue the person who caused the injury, and the court will decide whether that person is responsible and should pay damages. Many stories or make-believe scenarios can be used as the basis for a civil mock trial. In a civil trial, students are challenged to examine the effect of careless and hurtful behavior and recognize that sometimes the court will be asked to determine the consequences. There are some basic differences between civil and criminal trials; to help prepare students for a mock civil trial, some information on civil law is provided as follows.

Teacher Preparation: A Basic Introduction to Civil Law

A civil case is a matter between a person who has been injured, the plaintiff and the person who caused the injury, the defendant. Each of the parties involved hires lawyers to advise them on their legal rights and represent their case in court. A wrongful act that causes an injury may be both a crime and a civil wrong. A person who commits a criminal offense, such as an assault, will be prosecuted and the penalty may be jail time, but the victim is not compensated for their injuries in a criminal trial. The injured person would have to seek compensation in a civil trial for those injuries. But often the injury is caused by a careless rather than a criminal act. For example, a plaintiff may sue another driver for the injuries suffered in a car accident, or the plaintiff may sue a person for saying false and hurtful things about them. An individual can also sue a manufacturer whose product has caused them harm. For example, a woman successfully sued McDonalds, claiming they made their coffee too hot. When the coffee spilled on her, it caused a serious burn, and she was able to convince a court that McDonald's was at fault.

The plaintiff must prove that the defendant had a duty or responsibility to avoid harming the plaintiff; that he/she failed to live up to that duty; and that as a result of the failure the plaintiff suffered a tangible injury. The defendant tries to prove that there was no duty, or that if there was a duty that he/she acted at the standard expected of a reasonable person in the circumstances, or that the injuries were not a result of any careless act by the defendant. The judge decides whether the plaintiff has proven his/her case based on the balance of probabilities. This means that the judge listens to both sides, weighs the facts, and determines which side's story is more likely the truth. Depending on the decision, the judge will award compensation and costs against the defendant.

Most civil cases are heard by a judge alone. The judge will decide if the defendant should be held liable (responsible) for the injury and, if so, how much money the defendant should pay the plaintiff to compensate him/her for the injury. In some situations the plaintiff may think that a jury may be more sympathetic and will elect to have a jury. Having a jury always adds to the expense and time that it takes to hear a case. Because the loser in the case usually has to pay these costs, as well as any damages awarded to the plaintiff, most often the parties will opt for a judge alone. Because time and costs are not a factor in a mock trial, it is appropriate and more engaging to use a jury.

While the *Criminal Code of Canada* defines what constitutes a criminal act, there is no single code or law that identifies civil wrongs. Instead judges must refer to similar cases that have been decided in the past in other Canadian courts. An earlier case with similar facts is called a "precedent," and the judge in the present case must apply a similar decision.

Main Differences Between a Criminal Trial and a Civil Trial

Criminal Trial	Civil Trial
The accused must be found guilty beyond a reasonable doubt.	The judge decides whether the plaintiff has proven his/her case on the balance of probabilities.
There is a lawyer involved representing the government (called the Crown counsel or prosecution).	There is no Crown counsel (prosecution). Instead the plaintiff and defendant hire private lawyers.
The accused is either found guilty or not guilty.	The defendant is either found either liable or not liable and the court awards damages.
The jury has 12 members.	Often there is no jury. If a jury is used, it has 8 members.
Only the government can prosecute criminal cases.	Any person who has suffered an injury can file a civil lawsuit in court.

Choosing a Story or Scenario

The first step to organizing a civil mock trial is to identify an incident where a civil wrong has taken place. A number of scenarios lend themselves to civil law suits. Perhaps someone slipped and fell on a slippery floor and wants to sue the store. Or perhaps someone wants to sue another person for spreading false rumors about him/her, or perhaps a person has found a snail in his/her pop bottle.

Many of the stories discussed in this book include examples of wrongful behavior that can be dealt with by the civil court. For example, the three little pigs could sue the wolf for the loss of their homes. The bears could sue Goldilocks for breaking their furniture, and the Queen could sue Alice for damaging her garden. Chapter 10 contains a number of story ideas for developing a civil mock trial. When a story or scenario has been selected, the class must agree on the complaints that will form the basis of the civil suit, including the specific nature of the case against the defendant.

Civil Trial Procedure

In a civil trial, the lawyers and their clients sit at tables facing the judge. The court clerk and court reporter sit at a table in front of the judge. You can use the following as a black-line master to outline for the class the process in a civil court hearing.

The court clerk stands and announces the arrival of the judge: "Order in the Court. All rise." Everyone remains standing until the jury enters, and then the judge enters and takes his/her seat. The clerk then says, "This court is now in session. My Lord/My Lady Judge _____ presiding."

1. The plaintiff's counsel and the defendant's counsel introduce themselves to the judge, giving their full names.

2. The plaintiff's counsel begins with an opening statement, which describes the complaint and the injuries suffered by the plaintiff and mentions the evidence that will be presented to support the plaintiff's claim.

3. The plaintiff's counsel calls the plaintiff's witnesses one at a time and questions them about what happened.

4. After each witness has testified, the defendant's counsel cross-examines the plaintiff's witnesses, asking questions for the purpose of casting doubt or discrediting the statements made by them.

5. After all of the plaintiff's witnesses have testified, the defendant's counsel makes an opening statement describing the case for the defendant and describing what the defendant's witnesses will prove. The defendant's witnesses will try to show that the defendant had no responsibility for the injury or the injury was less serious than the plaintiff is claiming.

6. The defendant's counsel then calls its witnesses one at a time and questions them about what happened. The defendant's counsel may also call on expert witnesses.

7. After each of the defendant's witnesses has testified, the plaintiff's counsel cross-examines them.

8. The plaintiff's counsel then summarizes the case for the plaintiff in a final statement to the jury.

9. The defendant's counsel summarizes the case for the defendant case in a final statement to the jury.

10. The judge explains to the jury that their job is to decide on the facts of the case. Was the plaintiff's injury a direct result of the actions of the defendant? Should the defendant be held liable for those injuries and, if so, what should be the amount of the award for the damages suffered?

11. The jury leaves to deliberate.

12. The jury returns and the judge asks if they have reached a verdict. The jury responds with the decision. If the jury has found in favor of the plaintiff, the jury may recommend an amount of damages. The judge thanks the jury members for their participation and dismisses them.

13. The judge reviews precedent cases, considers the findings of the jury, and reminds the court of his/her obligation to follow the law. The judge renders a decision and gives reasons. The judge considers the jury's recommendations for an award of damages and decides the amount.

14. Once the judge has completed his/her statement, the court clerk says: "This session of the Court is now adjourned. All rise." The judge and jury leave the courtroom.

An Example of a Civil Mock Trial:

Potter vs. Malfoy and Snape

Recommended for Grades 5 to 7

We have modified an incident from the popular *Harry Potter and the Philosopher's Stone* by J.K. Rowling to give the class an example of how to develop a case and organize a civil mock trial from a story.

Children may not appreciate the fact that when they fail to play by the rules and someone is injured because of it, they can be held responsible for that injury. This point can be made quite clearly by holding a civil mock trial in which Harry Potter claims that Draco Malfoy and Professor Snape intentionally harmed him during a Quidditch match. Now, Harry is not the sort of boy to turn to the courts to solve his problems at school, but knowing that he could, might help children understand that there may be legal consequences if their own actions on the playground harm another child, and also that the school has a legal responsibility to ensure the safety of every child.

The Story

Harry Potter is found to have a special talent for flying a broomstick, which makes him a great asset to the Gryffindor Quidditch team. The Gryffindor's main rivals, the Slytherins, are determined to remove Harry from one particular match. During the first game of the season, Harry is the Seeker for his team, and his job is to fly high above the match, avoid the other players, watch out for the Bludgers, and be the first to catch the Golden Snitch. The team that captures the Golden Snitch is the winner of the game.

While Harry is cruising above the game, his broomstick suddenly veers out of control, and he has a difficult time holding on. Fortunately, his friends Ron and Hermione notice that Professor Snape (an employee of the Hogwarts School and the faculty advisor for the Slytherins) is concentrating very hard on Harry, and they are sure he is the cause of the trouble by casting some sort of spell. Hermione manages to distract Professor Snape and break the curse that he has put on Harry's broom.

For the purposes of this civil trial, let's alter the story somewhat. Suppose that Malfoy (Harry's nemesis) was playing on the Slytherin team. What if Malfoy took advantage of Harry's inability to control his broom and intentionally rammed Harry from behind causing him to fall to the ground? We might assume that Harry was knocked unconscious, broke his arm, and suffered severe bruising to his body. (Experts on the Harry Potter stories will realize that we have stretched the plot for the sake of creating an assault claim against the defendants. Teachers may find it necessary to alter the plot of any story to create reasonable grounds for a legal action.)

Let's suppose Harry decides to sue Malfoy for failing to follow the rules of the game and to sue Professor Snape for putting a curse on him, which is against school policy. The teacher can have the class hold the trial Harry vs. Malfoy and Professor Snape.

Preparing for the Trial

Divide the class into three teams: the Gryffindors for the plaintiff, the Slytherins for the defendants, and the Hufflepuffs as the court personnel and media team. For fun, the teacher could assign students to groups by drawing their names from a Sorting Hat, but it may also be appropriate to assign students to teams to ensure an equal balance of strengths among the groups. Because of the special circumstances of this case, the class may decide to hold the trial not in a courtroom but in the Great Hall of Hogwarts School.

Group 1: The Plaintiff's Team

The plaintiff: Harry Potter
Lawyers for the plaintiff (3 lawyers)
Witnesses for the plaintiff (witnesses could include Ron and Hermione; Oliver Wood, the Quidditch team captain; and Madam Hooch, the game referee)
An information sheet for this group follows.

Group 2: The Defendants' Team

The defendants: Draco Malfoy and Professor Snape
Lawyers for the defendants (3 lawyers)
Witnesses for the defendants: (witnesses could include Professor Dumbledor and members of the Slytherin Quidditch team)
An information sheet for this group follows.

Group 3: Court Personnel and Media Team

Sheriff, court clerk, and court reporter, court artist, newspaper journalist, television reporter, and members of the jury (a jury for a civil trial consists of eight people, but the size of the jury for the mock trial can be flexible, depending on the size of the class and on whether another class or parents will serve as jury members)
Refer to chapter 3 for role cards for this group. Role cards for judge and jury in this case follow.

As the students work with their groups to prepare for the trial, there are a number of things the teacher can do to provide support.

• Remind witnesses that they should try to maintain consistency with the story and prepare to give their responses to the lawyers' questions in character.

• Assist students with finding additional information and resources.

• Monitor the work of each team and each member of the team (for example, you could ask each student to keep a journal of group and individual activities).

• Arrange for a judge to preside at the trial.

Working in their teams, the plaintiff and defendant teams will study the incident in the story, extracting information necessary to support their case.

Information Sheet for the Plaintiff's Counsel

Plaintiff: Harry Potter

As a registered player on a school sports team participating in a game sponsored by the school, Harry Potter had a reasonable expectation that all the players would obey the rules of the game. When Malfoy hit Harry from the rear and dislodged him from his broom, he was acting beyond the rules of the game. The assault was intentional and it was the direct cause of Harry's injury. Professor Snape, as an employee of the school, knew that he was using his wizard powers inappropriately when he put a curse on Harry's broom. He created a situation in which Harry was unable to defend himself from Malfoy's attack thereby contributing to Harry's injuries.

It may be (although this will be difficult to prove) that Snape and Malfoy conspired to eliminate Harry from the match. At the least, as a supporter of the opposing team, Snape was negligent in his duties to Harry, to both teams, and to the school. On the principle of vicarious liability, Hogwarts School is liable because they did not adequately supervise the game or control the actions of the players or their employee, Professor Snape.

Gathering Evidence

The plaintiff's counsel will need to examine the novel to find all evidence that will support the plaintiff's position during the trial. To prepare for the trial, counsel will need to interview witnesses from both sides. All witnesses have a duty to tell the truth. They cannot later change their stories in court or they risk being charged with perjury or found in contempt of court. If this occurs, their testimonies will be struck down. The plaintiff's counsel can instruct witnesses for the plaintiff about what information they should or shouldn't provide to the court.

Preparing Questions

The plaintiff's counsel will want to prepare a strategy for questioning witnesses that will persuade the court that the plaintiff's version of the incidents that led to the injury are most likely true. One lawyer on the plaintiff's team needs to prepare an opening statement to describe briefly for the court what happened from Harry's perspective and then outline to the jury legal arguments the team will introduce to support the case. Another member of the legal team needs to prepare a closing statement that summarizes the arguments made by the plaintiff's side.

As the team prepares questions for the trial, keep in mind that lawyers should never ask a question their own witness cannot answer. It is not the lawyer's job to try to trick the witnesses. During the trial, lawyers for the plaintiff also cannot ask the plaintiff's witnesses leading questions, or questions that suggest a particular answer. An example of a leading question is "You saw Malfoy hit Harry, didn't you?" Instead, a more appropriate question would be: "Did you see Harry fall?" "What caused him to fall?"

When the plaintiff's lawyers cross-examine the witnesses for the defendants, they can ask leading questions. But if a lawyer for the defendants asks an inappropriate question, the plaintiff's lawyer can object. The judge must decide whether to sustain the objection – in which case the lawyer would have to rephrase the question – or to overrule the objection and allow the question.

Plaintiff's Witness Oliver Wood

As the Quidditch team captain, Oliver Wood could be asked to explain the rules of the game and describe what is considered unacceptable conduct for players. He could also describe the attack by Malfoy and its consequences. He might also be asked to testify about the history of animosity between the two teams.

Plaintiff's Witnesses Ron and Hermione

Ron and Hermione may be asked to describe what Professor Snape was doing in the stands during the game and how they finally managed to stop him from using the curse.

Any other concrete evidence that can be derived from the book may be added to the witnesses' testimonies.

Information Sheet for the Defendants' Team

Defendants: Draco Malfoy and Professor Snape

Hogwarts School is a unique school with the sole purpose of teaching witch-craft and wizardry. In order to accomplish this goal, students have to learn and practise those skills. Quidditch is a game that helps the students to achieve the necessary skills. No student is compelled to play. Students play voluntarily, and therefore, consent to injuries that might result from a game that everyone acknowledges is rough and where there is always risk of injury.

As a member of the Slytherins, Draco Malfoy has a duty to protect the repu-tation of his team. Winning is important and Malfoy could argue that he was merely playing the game as it was intended to be played – that it is often rough and players expect to get hurt. Harry had consented to play and there-fore should expect to get hit. If he fell that is just part of the game.

Professor Snape's job at the school is to teach the art of placing curses on things and so it is reasonable that he might have been practising while at the game. He was only doing what he was hired to do. Harry contributed to his own injury because he was an inexperienced player and was flying beyond his capabilities when he fell off his stick. During his testimony, Snape could probably deny that he was using a curse as there is likely no hard evidence against him. He could claim that he was planning the next day's lesson rather than watching Harry. He could testify that a Nimbus broomstick is not as reliable as is advertised and that he has seen them malfunction before. (The jury, of course, would have to decide if this evidence is reliable.)

Gathering Evidence

The defendants' counsel will need to examine the novel to find all the evi-dence that will support the defendants' position during the trial. To prepare for the trial, the lawyers will interview the witnesses from both sides. All wit-nesses have a duty to tell the truth. They cannot later change their stories in court or they risk being charged with perjury or found in contempt of court. If this occurs, their testimonies will be struck down. The defendants' counsel can instruct witnesses for the defendant about what information they should or shouldn't provide to the court.

Preparing Questions

The defendants' counsel will want to prepare a strategy for questioning wit-nesses that will persuade the court that the defendants' version of the inci-dents that led to the injury are most likely true. One lawyer on the defen-dants' team needs to prepare an opening statement to describe briefly for the court what happened from the defendants' perspective and then outline to the jury legal arguments the team will introduce to support the case. Another member of the legal team needs to prepare a closing statement that summa-rizes the arguments made by the defendants' side.

As the team prepares questions for the trial, keep in mind that lawyers should never ask a question the witness cannot answer. It is not the lawyer's job to try to trick the witnesses. During the trial, lawyers for the defendant also cannot ask the defendants' witnesses leading questions, or questions that suggest a particular answer. An example of a leading question is "You know that Harry is inexperienced at playing Quidditch, don't you?" Instead, a more appropriate question would be: "How often has Harry played Quidditch? Has he ever won before?"

When the defendants' lawyers cross-examine the witnesses for the defendants, they can ask leading questions. But if a lawyer for the plaintiff asks an inappropriate question, the defendants' lawyer can object. The judge must decide whether to sustain the objection – in which case the lawyer would have to rephrase the question – or to overrule the objection and allow the question.

Defendant's Witness Professor Dumbledor

As principal of the school, Professor Dumbledor must be ready to justify the kinds of activities he allows at the school, as well as the educational value of games such as Quidditch. He must assure the court that the game is well supervised and support Snape's argument that he did not use his wizard powers inappropriately.

Any other concrete evidence that can be derived from the book may be added to the witnesses' testimonies.

Information Sheet for the Jury

During the trial, jury members will listen and take notes. When the hearing is over they will decide which version of the story is most likely the most accurate account of what happened. They will decide whether the defendants should be held liable for Harry's injuries and, if so, how much money he should be awarded. Of course in a mock trial, the jury can also come up with a more creative penalty like Malfoy must publicly confess to deliberately causing Harry harm or Snape must teach Harry some special skills that only he knows.

The jury must not have made a decision about the case before hearing the arguments and witnesses, and the members must listen carefully to the evidence presented during the trial. The jury also needs to consider the legal principles and questions the judge presents. The jury must decide whether

- Snape and Malfoy conspired to harm Harry
- Malfoy's assault was intentional or accidental
- Harry consented to be hit
- The school should be held vicariously liable for the injury to Harry

After the witnesses have testified, the jury should take a preliminary vote on each question in turn. Then jury members can debate the merits of each question, try to get everyone to come to the same conclusions, and call for a final vote. In a civil case the vote of the majority constitutes the decision.

If the jury decides that Malfoy and Snape are liable, the jury then has to decide the degree of liability, and how Malfoy and Snape should compensate Harry.

Information Sheet for the Judge

The judge is responsible for managing the court procedure, hearing all the statements from both sides, listening to the witnesses and determining whether the lawyers' line of questioning is out of order or not. The judge also instructs the jury regarding procedure and law and makes the final decision after hearing their verdict.

Some Considerations about the Case

"Assault and battery" is any unwanted touching of someone in anger that causes injury. An important defense against assault is based on the principle of consent. It is generally acknowledged, for example, that a person playing in a dangerous sport consents to some physical contact. However, the contact must be within the rules of the game; a player does not consent to an unwarranted and violent attack. The jury must decide whether Malfoy's actions amounted to an assault and if so whether Harry consented to the degree of physical contact as part of the game. The jury must decide if the assault breached the rules of the game.

An employee of a school has a legal duty to look out for the best interests of all the students. He/she must do nothing to injure a student and must act reasonably to protect them from harm while they are on school property. The jury must decide if Snape conspired to harm Harry. If he did then his attack was intentional. The jury might also consider whether there was "aggravated assault," which means that there was malice on the part of one or both of the defendants and that a more serious result was intended.

An employer can be held liable for the intentional or careless acts of their employees. They must employ people who act with care and prudence. In the case of a school such as Hogwarts, school administrators must supervise their employees to be sure they follow school rules and policies. If they are negligent in the people they hire, or if they fail to control the behavior of their employees, the school and its directors can be held liable. This means they must pay for injuries caused by their employees.

In this case there may be direct liability because of the dangerous nature of the game and because the school did nothing to dispel the rivalry and hostility between the two teams. The jury must decide whether or not the school did enough to prevent the injury, whether the game was adequately supervised, and whether or not they knew or ought to have known that Snape and Malfoy intended to harm Harry.

The Law

If the jury's findings are dramatically inconsistent with other cases, the judge can reject the jury's findings. If the jury's findings are reasonable, however, the judge can affirm them and then make the final decision about the award of damages.

In a civil trial, decisions about damages are based on similar cases held in the past (called "precedents"). The Harry Potter case is similar to several actual lawsuits that determined liability for injuries in sporting events at schools. Here is a brief review of Canadian cases that could affect the decision in *Harry vs. Malfoy and Professor Snape*.

• In the case between two hockey players, Donald Brashear and Marty McSorly, the court decided that when McSorly hit Brashear on the head with his stick he acted beyond the rules of the game. McSorly had to compensate Brashear for his injuries and for the time he was unable to play because of them.

• In another case, a student injured in a snow boarding accident while he was on a school field trip was awarded compensation from the school district that employed the teachers. The teachers were found to be negligent because they did not adequately supervise the students on the ski hill.

• In another case, a high school basketball player who experienced extreme harassment from players on an opposing team successfully sued the school principal and school board because they did nothing to prevent or control the intense competitive rivalry that had developed between the schools and the players.

Debriefing

After the trial is over, the teacher should conduct a debriefing session to allow students to step out of their roles and talk about what they learned. Specific suggestions about the debriefing process are outlined in chapter 6. In this case, the class could relate the events and characters from this novel to similar circumstances in their own lives. The following are examples of questions that may be raised in the debriefing session.

- Did the trial provide a fair hearing of the matter?
- Was the trial a good way of resolving Harry's problem?
- Did the court get at the truth?
- What evidence or argument was most convincing to the jury?
- What have you learned about the law as a result of this mock trial?
- How does that knowledge affect your actions toward others?

Students' perceptions of the novel and its characters may change because of the mock trial. The teacher may want to explore these issues in more depth. Students could be asked questions such as

- Should the school bear some responsibility for the way Snape and Malfoy acted?
- Would it have been better for Harry just to ignore the assault and continue on as if nothing had happened?
- What other ways could this problem have been solved?
- What other legal issues can be found in the story?

Chapter 9: Conflict Resolution and Restorative Justice Activities: Other Ways to Solve Problems

While much of this book focuses on teaching issues of law and justice by simulating criminal or civil trials, it is critically important that children also understand that conflicts can be resolved in other ways. In this chapter, we examine different ways to solve problems and restore relationships, including mediation, negotiation, and justice circles.

The courts are not the only way or even the best way to solve problems. Going to court is expensive, formal, and time-consuming. Further, when people involved in a dispute turn over the problem and the decision to a third party, they can lose influence over the outcome. Because the courts are based on an adversarial model, people often come away from the process as enemies rather than friends. When preserving relationships and saving time and money are important, it is advantageous for people to consider other ways to solve problems, without resorting to court.

The activities in this chapter are designed to show positive and creative ways to resolve conflict and restore relationships. The skills that students practice in these activities, including communication, analysis, and creative thinking, can also be incorporated into daily life at school and reinforced as conflicts present themselves. If children can learn to stop a hurtful incident from escalating, assume responsibility for their own behavior, and expect others to do the same, they can move toward more cooperative relationships and build a stronger community. When children are encouraged to solve their relationship problems in positive and proactive ways, they are learning valuable skills for the future.

Chapter 3 includes warm-up activities that give students an opportunity to practise role play and experience the challenge of taking different points of view. It is helpful to involve students in these warm-up activities before having them undertake any of the more complex conflict resolution and restorative justice activities outlined in this chapter.

Negotiation

Negotiation takes place when two individuals or parties come together, clarify their problem, identify key issues, and express their opinions about how they think the conflict should be resolved. Both parties agree to make concessions until they reach a consensus so that they both go away satisfied with the outcome of the negotiation. Negotiation should always be one of the first steps individuals try when they have a difference that may lead to the breakdown of a relationship.

Ideally, negotiation takes place before a crime or civil wrong takes place. For example, if a person is annoyed by a neighbor's barking dog, it is better to negotiate a resolution with the dog's owner rather than take drastic action against the dog. Or, to use a fairytale as an example, perhaps Hansel and Gretel's father could have negotiated a better solution for his children with the stepmother rather than feeling that he needed to abandon them in the woods. Goldilocks certainly could have worked out a better deal with the bears rather than having to face them in court.

People experience many difficulties in their relationships with each other, but it is important to remember that most conflicts we experience in life can be negotiated.

The following factors are important to a successful negotiation.

• Both sides need to be willing to talk and they must agree to meet voluntarily. No one can be forced into a negotiation.

• Both sides should be evenly balanced so that one side does not take advantage of the other side during the discussion. There can't be a wide difference in the strength or capacity for dialogue between the parties.

• The parties must have a sincere desire to solve the problem and both must understand that it is in their best interests to come to a solution. They must both agree that handing the problem over to someone else to solve might result in a less favorable solution for all.

Choosing a Story for a Negotiation Activity

Almost any story that has a conflict between two people or two groups can be used for a negotiation activity. If a crime is committed in the story, the teacher may wish to stop the story before this event takes place and suggest that the characters negotiate an alternate solution. Chapter 10 lists a number of story ideas that work for a negotiation activity.

Learning Outcomes

General learning outcomes for simulation and role play activities are described in the introduction to this book. In addition to those listed, there are specific outcomes associated with learning negotiation skills. Students who participate in a negotiation activity should be able to

• Demonstrate an understanding of the story and be able to relate it to personal experience.

• Assume the role of a character involved in a negotiation process.

• Recognize both sides of an issue, such as, in the story of the Lorax, the economic and social value of a natural resource, the dangers associated with inappropriate exploitation of the resource, and the importance of seeking a balance between economic needs and protection of the environment.

• Participate in a strategy to resolve problems where conflicting interests are present.

• Communicate feelings and concerns and assess recommendations in a balanced and fair way.

• Summarize and report on a social problem and suggest areas of compromise.

Negotiation Activity: The Lorax

Recommended for Grades 5 to 7

Sometimes a sincere effort to negotiate can prevent more serious problems from developing. That might have been the case in the story of *The Lorax,* by Dr. Seuss. This is the story of a happy and peaceful place full of beautiful Truffula trees with colorful feather-like leaves. A character called the Once-ler sees profit in cutting down the Truffula trees. In spite of warnings from the Lorax (a short, old prophet who speaks on behalf of the trees), the Once-ler begins to cut down the trees and develop his booming business of Thneed sweaters made from Truffula leaves. At first the money and prosperity that the new business generates seems like a good thing but before long the inhabitants of the area – the bar-ba-loots, the swomme-swans, and the humming-fish – are forced to leave because they can no longer survive. Then people begin to notice that their beautiful trees are being replaced with piles of trash and broken equipment. Eventually even the Once-ler's relatives vanish because their community is no longer a happy, beautiful, or productive place. The only one left is the Once-ler, who regrets the destruction he caused.

If the story is stopped part way through and the inhabitants of the area are brought together with the Once-ler and his family, perhaps they could reach a negotiated settlement and the story would end more positively.

Activity Guidelines

Preparing for the Negotiation

The teacher should begin this activity by reading *The Lorax* to the class. This popular book by Dr. Seuss is available on-line, at most libraries and bookstores. Make sure that students understand the issues in the story and the conflict that has precipitated this negotiation. Students will then simulate a negotiation process in order to reach a solution before the Lorax's environment is completely destroyed.

Choose one student to be the Lorax and one student to be the Once-ler. These two students will act as team leaders and primary spokespeople during the negotiation. Then divide the class into two teams: the Lorax team and the Once-ler team. Students in the Lorax team choose which character group they want to belong to: the Barb-ba-loots, Swommee-Swans, Humming-Fish, or Truffula environmentalists. Students in the Once-ler team choose which character group they want to belong to: the Once-ler's uncles and aunts, the Once-ler's brothers and sisters, Thneed retailers/consumers, and Thneed economists. A breakdown of the four groups in each team is below.

The Lorax Team	The Once-ler Team
The Lorax (team leader)	The Once-ler (team leader)
Bar-ba-loots (Lorax Group 1)	Once-ler's uncles and aunts (Once-ler Group 1)
Humming-Fish (Lorax Group 2)	Once-ler's brothers and sisters (Once-ler Group 2)
Swomme-Swans (Lorax Group 3)	Thneed consumers (Once-ler Group 3)
Truffula environmentalists (Lorax Group 4)	Thneed economists (Once-ler Group 4)

When all of the small groups are established, each group should make a sign, drawing, or simple costume that identifies their group. Then each group picks up their role card and works together to answer the questions on their role card.

Role Cards

Following are role cards outlining questions which each group need to complete in order to prepare for the negotiation.

Bar-ba-loots Role Card (Lorax Team, Group 1)

To prepare for your role in the negotiation, work in your small group to come up with answers to the following questions.

1. What is a Bar-ba-loot?

2. What do you like to do best?

3. What was your town like before the Once-lers came?

4. What is it like now?

5. How has the Once-ler's business affected your life?

6. What needs to happen for you to be happy again?

7. What are you willing to do to make things better?

Humming-Fish Role Card (Lorax Team, Group 2)

To prepare for your role in the negotiation, work in your small group to come up with answers to the following questions.

1. What is a Humming-Fish?

2. What do you like to do best?

3. What was your town like before the Once-lers came?

4. What is it like now?

5. How has the Once-ler's business affected your life?

6. What needs to happen for you to be happy again?

7. What are you willing to do to make things better?

Swomee-Swans Role Card (Lorax Team, Group 3)

To prepare for your roles in the negotiation, work in your small group to come up with answers to the following questions.

1. What is a Swomee-Swan?

2. What do you like to do best?

3. What was your town like before the Once-lers came?

4. What is it like now?

5. How has the Once-ler's business affected your life?

6. What needs to happen for you to be happy again?

7. What are you willing to do to make things better?

Truffula Environmentalist Role Card (Lorax Team, Group 4)

To prepare for your role in the negotiation, work in your group to come up with answers to the following questions.

1. What is a Truffula Tree?

2. Why is it special?

3. Why is it important to the Lorax?

4. What are the Once-lers doing to the trees?

5. What problems are the factories causing and how will those problems affect the Lorax?

6. What are you willing to do to make things better?

Once-ler's Uncles/Aunts Role Card (Once-ler Team, Group 1)

To prepare for your role in the negotiation, work in your group to come up with answers to the following questions.

1.. What was your life like before Once-ler started his new business?

2.. Describe your job in the Thneed business?

3.. Why do you think the Once-ler is the best guy ever?

4. What advantages do you have now that you have a good job?

5. Do you see any disadvantages to the Thneed business?

Once-ler's Brothers/Sisters Role Card (Once-ler Team, Group 2)

To prepare for your role in the negotiation, work in your group to come up with answers to the following questions.

1. What was your life like before Once-ler started his new business?

2. Describe your job in the Thneed business?

3. Why do you think the Once-ler is the best guy ever?

4. What advantages do you have now that you have a good job?

5. Do you see any disadvantages to the Thneed business?

Thneed Consumers Role Card (Once-ler Team, Group 3)

To prepare for your role in the negotiation, work in your group to come up with answers to the following questions.

1. What is Thneed and where does it come from?

2. What can you do with a Thneed?

3. What do your customers think of Thneeds?

4. What would happen to your store if people couldn't buy Thneeds any more?

5. How much are you willing to pay to keep Thneed products on your store shelves?

6. Are there any disadvantages to having the Thneed product readily available?

Thneed Economist Role Card (Once-ler Team, Group 4)

To prepare for your role in the negotiation, work in your group to come up with answers to the following questions.

1. How has Thneed production changed this town?

2. What are the benefits for the community?

3. Are there any disadvantages to the Thneed business?

4. Why is it important to keep the business going?

5. What will happen when the Truffula trees are all gone?

6. What steps should be taken to save the Truffula Trees?

Team Meetings

After each character group has answered the questions in their role card, the Lorax team members meet together, and the Once-ler team meets together. (Each team should be in a separate area and out of ear-shot of each other.) During the team meeting, each of the groups share their concerns or the benefits they have achieved because of the Once-ler's actions. At the end of the discussion:

• The Lorax team (chaired by the Lorax) prepare a joint list of five things that they want changed in order to make their lives better.

• The Once-ler team (chaired by the Once-ler) prepare a joint list of five things that they are unwilling to give up now that their lives are better.

At this stage of the process, the two teams do not share any information with each other.

The Negotiation

For the negotiation, the Lorax team and Once-ler team will sit on opposite sides of the room, facing each other. Participants will be grouped along each line, in their small groups, with their group sign or costumes clearly visible. The teacher will serve as moderator for the negotiation, ensuring both sides have equal opportunities to share their point of view.

Before beginning, the moderator should convey the rules.

• Everyone takes a turn.

• Only one person speaks at a time.

• If a question is asked of one team, they must be given the chance to answer.

The negotiation will follow this format:

• One person from each of the four character groups on the Lorax side (Bar-ba-loots, Humming-Fish, Swomme-Swans, and Truffula environmentalist) makes a brief statement summarizing the problem from their perspective (1 min. each).

• The Lorax team leader concludes this presentation by presenting the five things they want changed in order to make life better for the Lorax.

• Then, one person from each of the four character groups on the Once-ler side (Aunts and Uncles, Brothers and Sisters, Thneed consumers, and Thneed economist) makes a brief statement summarizing what they have gained from their perspective (1 min. each).

• The Once-ler team leader concludes this presentation by presenting the five things they are unwilling to give up because their lives are better now than they were before.

• The teacher chairs a discussion period when representatives from one side can ask questions of the other side. The idea is to understand the other's perspective and to try to come to a solution that benefits all.

• The negotiation takes a recess, and the two teams then meet separately with their members to discuss what they heard and what they are willing to give up or change in order to find a solution. The teams review their list of demands and by the end of the discussion, each team should come up with a new list of what they want and what they are willing to give up in order to make the community a better place for all who live there.

Reaching a Settlement

• The teams re-assemble in the room facing each other, and the Lorax presents the Lorax team's proposal for a solution. The Once-ler team leader then presents the Once-ler's proposal for a solution. The teacher then chairs a discussion with one team asking questions of the other.

• If a joint decision cannot be reached between the two teams at this time, the teacher will ask the team leaders for the Lorax and the Once-ler to meet together privately to work out a mutually agreeable solution.

• The team leaders then meet back with their teams, present the proposal and the team members vote on it. If more than 50 percent of the members agree from both teams, then the settlement is reached and the simulation is over. If fewer than 50 percent agree, then the team leaders must meet again and try to find a better solution that suits the members.

Debriefing

The goal of the negotiation has been is to create an environment where both the residents and the business people can work and live together harmoniously. Students should discuss the process and consider the following questions.

• Has the negotiation achieved the goal of achieving harmony in the community?

• If not, why not? If so, explain.

• What will be required to make the agreement work?

• Can the Lorax and the Once-lers live happily ever after?

• What other things might be done to restore the relationship?

• How is this story like a situation in your own neighborhood, school, or community?

• What do you think about the process of negotiation?

• What skills did you learn in the process?

• How did you feel during the discussion and negotiation?

• What would happen in a negotiation if one side had more people or presented stronger arguments?

• Are negotiated settlements always fair?

• What would make for a fair settlement?

• In what circumstances would a negotiation be better than a trial?

• What happens if a member doesn't agree with that his/her representative negotiated? Are there any other options?

• What might have been an alternative way of arriving at a solution, rather than through a negotiation?

Evaluation Measures

Teachers can use different methods to evaluate students' work in the negotiation, based on both their individual and group written and oral responses. For example, teachers can assess how students carry out the following tasks:

• Relate the story in their own words.

• Create a list of the various individuals affected by the business and describe the effect the problems have had on each of them.

• Respond thoroughly to role card questions

• Participate in the negotiation process.

• Ask good questions and listen to the responses.

• Assimilate the needs and expectations of others.

• Appreciate each point of view

• Compromise until an agreement is reached.

• Work in groups, listening to each other and weighing ideas.

• Synthesize ideas into recommendations.

Note: It is possible to simplify the negotiation process for younger children. One alternate negotiation activity is to discuss the positions of the main characters in *The Lorax* and then ask students to align themselves with one of the sides represented in the story. Ask the students to work together as a group to build a case justifying their respective positions and articulate their views to the opposing side in an open forum. After the forum, ask the two sides to come to a consensus to resolve the conflict.

Mediation

Sometimes simple negotiation won't solve people's problems. If people are angry with one another, are unwilling to cooperate, or fear that they will be taken advantage of, it is better to set up a mediated settlement. In mediation the parties involved in a dispute agree to have a neutral person (the mediator) facilitate their discussion and help them reach a conclusion. Both sides need to agree on who should act as mediator. Then the mediator should speak with each side privately, finding out what their complaints are, what they need to solve the problem, and what concessions they are willing to make. The mediator then shares that information with the other side and suggests things that each side might do to come to a fair settlement. Mediation is essentially a private process, usually with only three parties involved – the mediator and the two people (or groups) involved in the conflict.

Peer mediation can be an effective way for students to resolve their own disputes in the classroom. After students have practised a mediation activity such as the one described below, the teacher could consider setting up a peer mediation program.

Choosing a Story for a Mediation Activity

Almost any story that has a conflict between two people (or two groups) could be used for a mediation activity. Chapter 10 lists a number of stories which present a problem that could be solved with the help of a mediator, if the characters can be persuaded to be reasonable and if the damage or injury caused can be undone or the parties can be compensated. Sometimes a story is best stopped in the middle, so that students can find their own solution to the problems presented before learning how the story actually ends.

Learning Outcomes

After participating in a mediation activity students should be able to:

• Identify and distinguish between legal problems that need to be resolved by a court and problems that might be resolved by mediation.

• Assume the role of a person involved in a dispute.

• Summarize their position and suggest areas of compromise.

• Participate in a strategy to resolve problems involving conflict.

• Communicate their feelings and concerns about the issue and assess fairly the recommendations developed.

• Compromise and negotiate.

• Synthesize perspectives into a mediated settlement.

Mediation Activity: Jack and the Beanstalk

Recommended for Grades 3 to 7

A well-loved English folktale, Jack and the Beanstalk is the story of a poor and starving boy named Jack, who lives on a farm with his widowed mother and their cow. Because they are so desperate for food and money, Jack's mother orders Jack to sell their cow, even though it is their only source of milk. On the way to the market, Jack meets a funny looking old man who convinces him to sell the cow for a handful of strange looking beans. His mother is furious, but Jack decides to plant the bean seeds before going to bed, and the next morning he discovers a giant beanstalk has grown from the beans. Jack climbs the beanstalk and arrives at the palace of the wealthy Giant, situated upon a cloud at the top of the beanstalk. While hiding in the Giant's home, Jack notices a bag of gold. After the Giant falls asleep, Jack grabs the gold and quickly climbs down the beanstalk. The Giant is enraged that he's been robbed, but Jack and his mother use the gold to live very well for a long time. When the gold runs out, Jack climbs the beanstalk to try his luck again. This time, he spots the Giant's hen, who lays golden eggs. While the Giant sleeps, Jack grabs the hen and the egg and returns home to his mother with the new riches.

In the traditional version of this story, Jack returns to the Giant's home a third time and, while the Giant sleeps, steals the Giant's golden harp. This time, however, the Giant wakes up and begins to chase Jack down the beanstalk. Jack quickly chops down the beanstalk and the Giant falls to his death. For this mediation activity the teacher can either stop the story before Jack cuts down the beanstalk and kills the Giant or else modify the story so that the Giant survives his fall from the beanstalk.

Activity Guidelines

• Read Jack and the Beanstalk to the class and discuss the issues and conflicts in the story.

• Ask the class to decide what issue requires mediation. For example, the Giant's perspective is that he is angry that his bag of gold and hen that lays the golden eggs are missing and he wants them back. According to Jack, he and his mother are poor and the Giant is wealthy, so the Giant should be willing to share.

• Divide the class into small groups of three students each: one will play Jack, one the Giant, and one the mediator.

• Students playing Jack and students playing the Giant work independently to build their case. They each need to identify their complaint, describe the problem from their character's perspective, and create a list of what they want.

• The mediators read the Mediator's Guide. The mediators also review the story carefully, prepare a list of questions they want answered, and organize the mediation.

Mediator's Guide

The mediator's job is to help the two parties in a dispute solve their problem. You listen carefully and are encouraging but don't take sides. As mediator you don't tell either side what they should do and you do not blame anyone. Instead, your role is to help the people involved figure out the solution for themselves.

Introduction

You begin by welcoming the parties to mediation and explaining your role to them. Review the ground rules for the mediation, which include the following:

- They must tell the truth.
- They must listen when the other person is talking.
- They must try hard to solve the problem.
- Only one person speaks at a time. (No interrupting.)
- Indicate that they will have 40 minutes to reach an agreement.

Review the Story

Next you need to gather the main facts of the story from each person's point of view. You do this by following the steps below.

- Ask the Giant what happened.
- Summarize what the Giant says to make sure you understand.
- Ask Jack what happened.
- Summarize what Jack says to make sure you understand.
- Ask the Giant what the problem is and how he feels about the situation.
- Summarize what the Giant says.
- Ask Jack what the problem is and how he feels about the situation.
- Summarize what Jack says.
- If necessary, ask questions of either person (the Giant and Jack) to make sure you understand each person's perspective.
- Tell the Giant and Jack that they have five minutes to write down what they are willing to do to solve the problem. These suggestions are called "concessions" or "compromises."

Finding a Solution

- After five minutes, ask each party for their list of concessions.
- Read out loud each party's list of concessions.

• Encourage the Giant and Jack to discuss the options or to make further concessions until they come to a solution that they find acceptable. You may suggest some further compromises if it seems necessary. If needed, you can ask the Giant and Jack to rewrite their list of concessions if these have changed following the discussion.

• At the end of the second session, write what the parties have agreed to and encourage the Giant and Jack to sign that document, as proof that they have come to an agreement.

The mediation should last no longer than 40 minutes. Some groups may not have settled their differences during this time, but the teacher should still stop the process. During the debriefing session, the fact that the dispute was not settled in 40 minutes could be a point of discussion with all the students in the class.

Debriefing

Back in the full group, ask the mediators to summarize the outcome of their respective sessions and present to the class a brief description of the problem, the positions of the two disputants, and the agreement that they reached. If there was no agreement possible, the mediator should attempt to explain why. It is also interesting to discuss with students why different solutions were reached in the various groups and to speculate why these differences occurred.

Ask the role players how it felt to be caught up in the midst of a disagreement, how it felt to discuss it with a neutral person and make compromises, and what it meant to them to be able to resolve (or not resolve) the problem.

Give students the opportunity to comment on whether they thought the process was worthwhile, whether they felt that they had retained control of the situation, and how they now felt about the character with whom they had their dispute.

Invite all members of the class to respond to questions about the effectiveness of the strategy and how it might be applied to solve their own disputes in school or in the community.

Evaluation Measures

Students may be evaluated on the basis of their individual and group written and oral responses as they:

• Adopt a character role and identify the elements of the story that affect that character.

• Summarize the problems in the story that require resolution.

• Articulate a point of view orally and in writing.

• Listen to others and respond in a reasonable fashion.

• Demonstrate their skill in facilitating a simulated mediation.

• Demonstrate their capacity to make compromises and come to a fair agreement.

• Synthesize information into an equitable solution.

Restorative Justice

Restorative justice is a process that brings parties together in a resolution process that tries to meet the needs of everyone involved. It aims to heal the wounds of the victims, rehabilitate offenders, and deal with social problems in communities. A justice circle is a strategy used in many aboriginal communities in Canada, and is one example of restorative justice. If a First Nations' person is convicted of an offence by the courts, the judge may decide the offender can be sentenced by his/her peers or the community rather than receiving a conventional sentence of a fine or prison. The offender is turned over to a sentencing circle or justice circle, comprised of a provincial or territorial court judge and members of the offender's community, including the victims.

In a justice circle a group of people from the community gather together to deal with the offender and address the effect his/her crime has had on the victim and the community. Everyone who has been affected by a particular offence – the offender, his or her family, the victims, and the victim's representatives – work together to try to agree on a fair and reasonable way for the offender to account for his/her actions and compensate the victims for the injury. An aim of the justice circle is to shift the objective of sentencing away from punishment toward accountability, rehabilitation, and restitution. It is an attempt to restore relationships between parties and to be a step in building a stronger and more harmonious community.

All participants in the justice circle sit together to discuss the impact the offense had on the different members of the community, the sentence that would be most appropriate for the offender and what it would take to help the community heal from the offence. In the presence of respected community members, elders, peers, the victim, and the victim's family, the offender is presented with statements from the victim and the family explaining the effect of his/her actions on their lives. The justice circle encourages the offender to acknowledge the harm he/she has done to the victims and allows the community to share the responsibility of making things better.

The classroom is an ideal place to simulate a justice circle. Because a justice circle simulation acknowledges differences between people, encourages communication and fosters a sense of community, it enhances cooperative and harmonious relationships among the students in the class. Stepping into the role of offenders, victims, and community members, the students are encouraged to be more sensitive and less judgmental. The experience requires them to look beyond the immediate problem and propose solutions that will heal rifts and foster positive social values.

The roles that students play in a justice circle can be fictional characters or real people. A justice circle may be based on a crime committed in a story or fantasy tale, or the teacher may wish to choose an actual event or a news report. A hypothetical scenario or case study could be created that students can relate to and share in the process of resolving. The main condition for selecting a story or situation is that students are able to relate to the crime and imagine the community in which the victim and offender live. In the scenario presented here, a case study example is offered that is more realistic than imaginary.

Learning Outcomes

After participating in a circle justice activity students should be able to:

• Appreciate the impact of a criminal offence on a community.

• Participate in a forum that confronts an offender.

• Present a point of view and argue a position.

• Assume a role and convey relevant information.

• Clearly articulate a position in a short time.

• Listen to and respond to a variety of perspectives.

• Balance the needs of several players and come to a fair solution.

• Develop ideas on how to compensate the victims fairly.

- Suggest ways that an offender may be rehabilitated and reintegrated back into a community.

- Initiate a process of healing and renewal for both the offender and the community.

- Become more familiar with the notion of restorative justice and the benefits of this approach to problem solving.

Justice Circle Activity: Vandalizing the Playground

Recommended for Grades 5 to 7

Time required: Planning and holding a justice circle usually involves three separate sessions: session 1: becoming familiar with the justice circle and the case, session 2: identifying and planning the roles, and session 3: enacting the justice circle. The teacher should allow about 45 to 60 minutes for each session. Ideally these sessions should be on consecutive days.

One evening in early spring three 14-year-old boys met at their favourite hangout. Because there wasn't a lot for the boys to do that night, they thought it was a good idea when one of them suggested they go hang out at the playground at their old elementary school. At the playground the boys played on swings that were too small for them and, as a result, they damaged the seats. They jumped on the ends of the teeter-totters until one of the boards broke. This damage got the boys really excited and so together they pushed over the slide, bent the monkey bars, and punched holes in the bouncing equipment. When they realized the damage they had caused, they tried to cover it up by dumping the contents of the schoolyard's garbage containers onto the playground. When they finished, the boys' excitement began to diminish as they realized what they had done. They went to their homes hoping that no one had seen them or could connect them with the mess they had left behind.

The next morning the damage was discovered first by the children who arrived to play before school and then by the school principal, who called the police. When the police interviewed the neighbors, some of them reported that they saw teenage boys playing on the grounds the previous night. One of the neighbors was able to identify the boys. The police went to the boys' homes to question them about the vandalism. At first each boy denied knowing anything about the playground, but after much questioning, the truth came out and each boy admitted to causing the damage.

Taking into account that the boys are young and that this is their first offence, the police go to the principal of the elementary school to consult with her about what action to take. Because the boys had been students at the school a few years before, the principal thinks that the school should play a role in determining what happens and how the boys should be punished. She decides that an older class at the elementary school should organize a justice circle to consider what should happen to the boys. The principal says that she will take into consideration the decision of the circle when she makes her recommendation to the police on how to deal with the young offenders.

Activity Guide

In this activity, the class has the assignment of conducting the justice circle.

Session 1: Becoming Familiar with the Justice Circle and the Case

In this introductory session, students learn about the nature and purpose of a justice circle, the procedures involved, and the benefits of this approach to problem solving. Students are also introduced to the vandalism story.

Before choosing a role to enact in the justice circle, students should suggest people who may be affected by this incident. They should give each boy a name, develop personality traits, and imagine their family situations, their experiences, and suggest what might have motivated them to do this. Students should be encouraged to think about the situation from the boys' perspective and consider their circumstances. Perhaps one boy was new to the neighborhood and gave in easily to peer pressure because he wanted to fit in. Perhaps one of the boys had been bullied at school and this was his way of feeling powerful. Perhaps one of the boys parents were rarely home and he had no supervision. The teacher should work with the class to create a reasonable character for each of the boys. This process helps the students relate to the boys and identify with their situation.

During this discussion, students also need to determine the damage the boys caused, including the cost of cleaning up, replacing the school playground equipment, and installing security measures to prevent further vandalism. The teacher should also help the class consider the fact that many of the young children who saw the damage may have felt considerable fear about what they saw in their "safe" playground, or what they think could happen in other environments that they considered safe.

Session 2: Identifying and Planning the Roles

In this session, the class suggests who should be involved in the justice circle. It could include the boys, the boys' parents, former or current teachers, social workers, friends of the boys, children who were affected by the boys' actions, the police officers who interviewed the boys, neighbors who live near the school, and teachers or playground supervisors at the school. Have each student choose a role (all different) and prepare notes from the case scenario and from the class discussion. Each student should also prepare a role card on the role he/she is playing.

The students can consider the following questions as they develop a position on the case from the perspective of the character they are going to play:

- What is their relationship to the boys? Do they know them all or just one or two of them?

- How long have they known the boys?

- What responsibilities have they had toward the boys?

- Have they measured up to those responsibilities?

- What do they think prompted the action at the playground?

- Do they think any or all of the boys would commit such an act again?

- What was the impact of the boys' actions on them?

- What do they think should be done now?

- What role could they play in working towards a solution?

• How can the boys pay for the damage caused and the effect of their actions on others?

Before students begin preparing for their role for the justice circle, remind them that the purpose of the circle is to decide what should be done about the crime. Everyone participating in the circle should be prepared to speak about the effect of the crime on the school, the children at the school, and the community as a whole. Each of the boys should be given the opportunity to apologize, if that is his feeling, and explain what prompted the offence. It is hoped that they will also state that they will try hard not to re-offend. The boys' parents might accept some responsibility, and they may want to explain that their child is usually a good person who has many redeeming qualities or is truly remorseful. They may also add some insights about their child, which may shed some light on the case. The purpose is to try to come to an equitable or just solution that all participants can support.

Session 3: Enacting the Justice Circle

In this session, students follow the procedure of the justice circle, with each student in role sharing the effect of the offence on him/her. When all individuals have shared their thoughts, the group will come to a decision about what should happen to the boys. Once the roleplay is over the teacher will debrief with the students.

To hold the justice circle, arrange the classroom into a large circle of chairs. All justice circles have a judge, who facilitates the circle and ensures the process remains orderly. The teacher is usually the best person to take on this role. A talking stick is often used in First Nations' culture to ensure that only one person speaks at a time, and the class may want to use a talking stick or other symbolic object to help control the discussion process.

The judge formally introduces the purpose of the circle, letting the students know that the results of the decision will influence the outcome of the case, because the principal will take their recommendations to the prosecutor in charge of the case against the boys. The group needs to be fair and reasonable and think of what is best for all the people involved – the boys, their families, their friends, their school, and its students. They also need to satisfy justice because our society believes it is important that people respect the law and that there will be consequences when people do wrong. They also need to think about the future of the boys and consider what could be done to deter them and others from vandalizing school property. It is hoped that the suggestions provided will help the boys turn their lives around and engage in more productive and positive activities.

In a justice circle, the victim and the victim's family and representatives are usually the first to speak. In this case, the victims are the children and the teachers at the school. They should be followed by others who have a stake in the outcome, and who may have been affected in some way by the offence. The offenders and their families and supporters speak last. As each person speaks, he/she holds the talking stick and no one else is allowed to talk until it is their turn to hold the talking stick. Each person should only speak for one to two minutes and should speak from notes they've prepared in advance.

After everyone has had a chance to speak, the judge briefly summarizes what has been learned from the participants. The judge then asks for comments from the victim's side and the offender's side about what punishment might be appropriate and how the victims and community can be compensated for the damage caused. Perhaps there is a different solution for each offender, or perhaps the group wishes to recommend the same outcome for each youth.

The judge tries to find common ground from all the suggestions and then suggests a solution that meets the needs of both sides. The group then votes on whether they can accept the suggestion. If not, they continue to make further recommendations until everyone is satisfied with the outcome. If no resolution is acceptable to everyone, the judge has the power to make the final decision, but the judge should only do this when other possible solutions have been exhausted.

Debriefing

After a decision has been made and the circle is dissolved, the teacher should help the students debrief by asking each student how they felt about the person they represented. Students can also share their ideas about the justice circle process. This discussion can be held on the following day. Below are some suggested questions to ask students:

• Is this method of dealing with a problem fair to the parties involved?

• Would this resolution process help a community heal from the effects of an offence or will it lead to more hurt?

• Would an offender be helped by this process or would he/she be likely to commit another offence?

• Would a victim be helped by this process?

• What are the negative and positive aspects of this process of deciding justice matters?

Evaluation Measures

The teacher can evaluate students based on:

• How they integrate the facts of the story into character roles and sentencing options.

• How they prepare their role cards and develop their character.

• How they portray their role in the justice circle.

• How clearly and persuasively they make their arguments during the justice circle.

• How well they understand the legal and personal consequences of damaging property.

• How well they exercise their listening skills.

• How well they can assimilate the information presented by the players into a workable solution.

• How well they compromise and negotiate an equitable solution.

• How effectively they prepare written reports of the outcome of the justice circle.

• How much clarity and detail they provide in their list of recommendations for the principal.

A Justice Circle Based on a Fairytale

A justice circle can be held using a conflict from a fairytale or storybook. For example students could do a justice circle for The Three Little Pigs. The book *The True Story of The Three Little Pigs,* by John Scieszka takes the perspective of the wolf who feels that the pigs' false accusations have ruined his reputation. A justice circle could be formed to determine whether the wolf's claims are justified and consider how their differences might be resolved.

Students representing the wolf, the three little pigs and the parents of the three little pigs plus others who play a role in the story can be asked to attend a justice circle and account for their words and actions. The wolf explains his threats and assaults on the pigs and provides character witnesses to attest to his good behavior. A social worker and probation officer can explain how they worked with the wolf and how effectively he had reformed his ways. But the circle also needs to hear from the pigs and their parents who suffered great emotional strain from the wolf's attacks. The participants in the circle work together to decide if the wolf has been the victim of defamation, or if he is guilty of the offence and what his punishment should be. The process of understanding the backgrounds of the offenders and victims and the facts of the incident, assessing the extent of the injury, determining guilt, and then agreeing on a reasonable conclusion to the case provide opportunities for students to practise the skills that will make them more responsible members of their communities.

Chapter 10: Story Ideas for Mock Trials and Other Activities

Stories that deal with legal and moral issues come from every corner of the world. In this chapter a few contemporary and multicultural storybooks are introduced that work well for a mock trial or a conflict resolution activity. Also included are comments on some of the legal issues, which can be found within the stories. All of these stories are also excellent resources for fruitful classroom discussions about legal concepts and principles.

Contemporary Stories

Crimi, Carolyn. Don't Need Friends. Illustrated by Lynn Munsinger. Dragonfly Books, 1999.

When Rat's best friend Possum moves to another junkyard, Rat decides he doesn't need friends. He refuses to become involved with Pigeon, Racoon, and the other animals in the community. One day, a big mean-looking dog moves in to Rat's neighborhood. Although they are determined not to be friends, Rat and Dog discover they need each other.

Issues: Can one live in isolation within a community of others? What laws come in to play when someone new moves in to an area where others have lived? What rules and laws impact on members of a community who do not get along? What are the rules of ownership? Did the other animals have legal ownership of their neighborhood in the junkyard before Dog came along? What civic rights and responsibilities do they have as members of this community?

Strategies: Role play the dilemma facing the animals in the junkyard and explore strategies for them to develop a supportive and inclusive community. Conduct a justice circle with the animals and try to engage Rat back into the community

Ering, Timothy Basil. The Story of Frog Belly Rat Bone. Cambridge, MA: Candlewick Press, 2003.

Cementland is grey and ugly. One day, a boy finds a special and mysterious treasure which promises to change Cementland into an enjoyable place. When thieves steal the treasure, he must come up with a creative plan to thwart them and save the treasure.

Issues: Based on the legal definitions of theft and possession, who does the treasure legally belong to? What punishment should the thieves face? What are the legal issues involved in the boy's plan to save the treasure? If the thieves have a change of heart, does that change their original guilt and therefore change the punishment? What are the rights and responsibilities of the citizens of Cementland? What are the legal issues of environmental protection involved?

Strategies: Discussion, mediation, negotiation, debates, criminal mock trial based on theft, or justice circle

Fox, Mem. Feathers and Fools. Illustrated by Nicholas Wilton. San Diego: Harcourt Brace, 1996.

This is a modern fable about some peacocks and swans who lived peacefully in neighboring communities, until they began to question and fear their differences.

Issues: This is a powerful story about assumptions and about the fear and misunderstanding of differences, which can destroy peace and lives. It is also a story of new hope and new beginnings based on tolerance, acceptance, and similarities. What are the social and legal obligations to seek the truth, and not defame others? What are the consequences of acting on supposition and innuendo?

Strategies: Discussion, debates, mediation, or negotiation

Karlins, Mark. Salmon Moon. Illustrated by Hans Poppel. New York: Simon & Schuster Books for Young Readers, 1993.

One day, while working in the fish market, Mr. Lutz comes across the most beautiful salmon he has ever seen, and it is still alive. Together, with his friends Mrs. Mankowitz and Sarah, they embark on a plan to rescue the salmon and set it free.

Issues: Is it ever acceptable to break the law (steal) for what you consider is a worthwhile cause? Could Sarah, Mr. Lutz, and Mrs. Mankowitz have achieved their goal in some other way, without breaking the law? How? Does "the end" justify "the means" – is it okay to use civil disobedience to support environmental issues?

Strategies: discussion, debates, criminal mock trial based on theft, letters to the editor

Kasza, Keiko. The Mightiest. New York: G.P. Putnam's Sons, 2003.

One day, Bear, Elephant, and Lion discover a golden crown deep in the forest. The crown is sitting on a rock. Inscribed on the rock are the following words: "For the Mightiest"! Their argument over who deserves the crown leads to dire consequences and an invaluable lesson.

Issues: Does our society exist through control by power and might, or is the rule of law dependent on an informed and socially responsible citizenry? Does a civilized society abide by the rules/laws through fear or enlightenment?

Strategies: Stop the story before the giant appears, and have a discussion or debate which animal is the mightiest and why. Finish the story and discuss what the animals have learned and how their new wisdom could be extended to enlighten the three new animals who are introduced on the last page of the story.

Levine, Arthur A. Pearl Moscowitz's Last Stand. Illustrated by Robert Roth. New York: Tambourine Books, 1993.

The neighborhood on Gingko Street has experienced many changes throughout the years. Friendships flourish as new families arrive from new cultures, but one by one, the cherished gingko trees have disappeared. When City Hall decides to remove the last tree, in the name of progress, Pearl Moskowitz gathers the community together to take a stand.

Issues: How can a community exercise democratic involvement and have a meaningful effect on civic decisions? Are there times when civil disobedience is the only option? Explore the issue of protection of the environment verses "progress."

Strategies: Discussion, mock trial based on civil disobedience, mediation or negotiation activities, role play to explore the effectiveness of initiatives such as petitions, speaking at City Hall meetings, and involving the media to get a message out

Muth, Jon J. The Three Questions. New York: Scholastic Press, 2002.

Based on a story by Leo Tolstoy, this is the story of young Nikolai, who searches for the answer to the three questions: When is the best time to do things? Who is the most important one? What is the right thing to do? Unable to find the answers from his three friends – Sonya, the heron; Gogol, the monkey; and Pushkin, the dog – Nikolai embarks on an adventure to find the answers by climbing to the top of the mountain where Leo, the wise turtle, lives. The answers lie within the actions Nikolai takes on his journey.

Issues: What are the legal, moral, and ethical issues of being a member of society, responsible to the needs of others? How can we be mindful of the effect of our own actions, and consequences of the decisions we make?

Strategies: Discussion; oral and written opinion pieces on the three questions. Debate the priority of each question – which is most important and why? Develop legal dilemmas around the third question: "What is the right thing to do?"

Phillips, Christopher. The Philosophers' Club. Illustrated by Kim Doner. Berkeley: Tricycle Press, 2001.

Which came first, the chicken or the egg? What is philosophy? What is violence? This is a book of questions, based on the Philosophers' Club format. It encourages creative and critical thinking skills, challenges opinions, extends perceptions, and develops reasoning skills.

Issues: Many of the questions included in this book can be discussed from a legal perspective. Questions include: What is violence? What is the difference between the truth and a lie? What do you think is the most important question you can ask?

Strategies: Discussion, debate, start a "Philosophers' Club."

Polacco, Patricia. Appelemando's Dreams. Philomel Books, 1991.

Applemando dreams beautiful, colorful dreams which his close friends can see in the air! Then one day, they discover that Applemando's dreams can be caught on wet paper and enjoyed as pictures. But when Applemando dreams on a rainy day and the entire town is covered in incredible pictures, the villagers become angry and accuse the children of playing a prank. They do not believe the children are telling the truth. As a fit punishment is discussed, a crisis occurs which results in the villagers coming to appreciate the power and beauty of Applemando's dreams.

Issues: What is vandalism? Is graffiti vandalism? What is an appropriate punishment for the crime of vandalism? Is "intent" necessary to be held accountable and found "guilty"? What can be done when others don't believe you are telling the truth? Can an illegal act have a positive consequence? What are the rights of property owners?

Strategies: Discussion, mediation, or negotiation activities; role play a "Town Hall" meeting between the children and the elders and debate both sides of the issue.

Wild, Margaret. Fox. Illustrated by Ron Brooks. La Jolla, CA: Kane/Miller Book Publishers, 2001.

An injured magpie and a one-eyed dog live happily together in the forest, until a jealous fox arrives to teach them what it means to be alone. Truth, courage, abandonment, responsibility, and deception are explored in the relationship of these three characters.

Issues: Who is more responsible for what happened: Dog for inviting Fox into their community, Magpie for abandoning Dog and not being satisfied with what she had, or Fox for tricking Magpie? Did Fox abandon Magpie and leave her to die? What could Fox be charged with legally? If a mock trial were held and Fox were charged, what would be the legal arguments for both sides? Would the result be different depending on whether Magpie finds her way back to her home with Dog or dies in the desert?

Strategies: Discussion, criminal mock trial, justice circle, mediation.

Wildsmith, Brian. The Owl and the Woodpecker. Oxford University Press, 1993.

The animals in the forest hold a meeting to try to resolve a problem between two members of their community who are fighting. Woodpecker is creating a noise during the day when Owl is trying to sleep. Neither of them will move. The peaceful life of the forest is being destroyed.

Issues: How does a community resolve a problem between two members who both think their side is right? Who has a legal right to stay? What legal obligations do the woodpecker and the owl have to do to preserve the peace? Discuss citizenship rights and responsibilities. Discuss noise bylaws and policies. Investigate land ownership issues. Explore the actions of each animal character in relation to the social responsibility skills of contributing to a group process, valuing diversity, exercising democratic rights and responsibilities, and solving problems.

Strategies: Discussion, debates, civil mock trial, mediation, or negotiation. Investigate municipal laws and policies; discuss personal rights verses the rights of the group as a whole.

Wildsmith, Brian Professor Noah's Spaceship. New York: Oxford University Press, 1992.

The animals of the forest, who have lived together happily, begin to notice that their environment is starting to change. The air is no longer easy to breathe, the water is no longer clean, and their habitat is being destroyed. They call a meeting and seek help from Professor Noah. Together, they save their planet.

Issues: This story examines the issues of exercising democratic rights and responsibilities and civic action, addressing environmental issues and the law, and working together as a group of committed citizens to address the problem rather than working as individuals. What other strategies could the animals have explored if they had not found Professor Noah?

Strategies: Discussion, civil mock trial, mediation or negotiation activities; extend the discussion into local environmental issues and explore environmental protection laws.

Wood, Douglas. Old Turtle and the Broken Truth. Illustrated by Jon J Muth. New York: Scholastic Press, 2003.

Earth is full of suffering and war until one little girl seeks Old Turtle, who tells her about a "broken truth" and how mending it will help her community understand the common bond of all humanity.

Issues: This story addresses the loss of rights and protections as a society and the weakening of the social fabric when legal and moral responsibilities are not recognized, valued, and exercised. It also considers the moral responsibility of each individual to the other citizens of the world.

Strategies: Discussion , justice circle.

Multicultural Stories

Alexander, Lloyd. The King's Fountain. Illustrated by Ezra Jack Keats. New York: E.P. Dutton and Co. Inc, 1971.

This is a Chinese story about a king who wants to build a huge fountain in his courtyard — even though filling it with water will mean that the village outside of the palace will have no water. A poor man tries to find someone wise, stronger, and cleverer than himself to persuade the king not to build the fountain.

Issues: Issues addressed include leadership, abuse of power, standing up against injustice, and individual versus majority rights.

Strategies: Discussion; civil trial around the issues of responsibility and negligence, mediation, or negotiation

Bailey, Lydia (retold by). Mei Ming and the Dragon's Daughter: A Chinese Folktale. Illustrated by Martin Springette. Richmond Hill, ON: North Winds Press, 1990.

Searching for a way to share her discovery of a mountain lake with her drought-stricken village, Mei Ming befriends the daughter of a dragon. With the help of the dragon's daughter, Mei Ming steals the key which releases the water from the dragon's control.

Issues: When is it morally right to break a law? This story also explores issues of property and ownership.

Strategies: Discussion; criminal mock trial based on theft, justice circle

Hamilton, Virginia. The Girl Who Spun Gold. Illustrated by Diane Dillon. New York: Blue Sky Press, 2000.

From the West Indies, The Girl Who Spun Gold is a retelling of Rumpelstiltskin. In this story, the protagonist, Quashiba, must decide to stay or to leave her husband, who has been very cruel to her.

Issues: This story examines issues related to divorce, relationships, physical abuse, and individual rights.

Strategies: Discussion; civil trial based on divorce and cruelty.

Hoban, Russell. The Dancing Tigers. Illustrated by David Gentleman. London: Jonathan Cape Publishers, 1979.

This is a story of a community of tigers who are in danger of being killed by the Rajah and his servants. The tigers must band together against the Rajah, to save their lives.

Issues: Issues examined include endangered species, environmental protection, environmental law, and the protection of animals.

Strategies: This story would work well for a mediation or negotiation activity.

Jaffe, Nina. Older Brother, Younger Brother: A Korean Folktale. Illustrations by Wenhai Ma. New York: Viking: 1995.

When a father dies, a greedy elder brother takes all of the father's property and refuses to share any of it with his younger brother (whom he banishes). Despite how badly he is treated, the younger brother is kind and generous – which shows the older brother the error of his ways.

Issues: This story addresses inheritance laws, cruelty, punishment, and fairness.

Strategies: Discussion, civil mock trial on inheritance laws, negotiation or mediation activity.

Miller, William. The Bus Ride. Illustrated by John Ward. New York: Lee & Low Books Inc., 1998.

This is the story of an African American girl and her mom who challenge an unjust law. Though they must sit at the back of the bus, one day the little girl moves up to the front – causing a huge discussion across the city. This story loosely based on Rosa Parks' historic decision not to give up her seat to a white passenger on a bus in Montgomery, Alabama, in 1955.

Issues: This story examines discrimination, racism, individual rights, and changing laws.

Strategies: Discussion of unjust laws; civil trial.

Munsch, Robert, and Micael Kusugat. A Promise is a Promise. Art by Vladyana Krykorka. Toronto: Annick Press, 1988.

After foolishly taunting and slandering the Qallupilluq who live under the ice, a little Inuit girl outsmarts the dangerous creatures to regain her freedom.

Issues: This story examines defamation and slander.

Strategies: Discussion; civil trial on defamation and slander.

Paterson, Katherine. The Tale of the Mandarin Ducks. Lodestar: 1990.

This is a Japanese story about two servants who help to save a mandarin duck from a greedy lord. The servants are sentenced to death when they set the duck free, but the duck and his mate reward the kind servants by outwitting the lord.

Issues: This story examines animal rights (holding creatures captive), greediness, sharing, and honoring kind acts.

Strategies: Discussion; criminal trial based on cruelty to animals.

Patron, Susan. Burgoo Stew. Illustrated by Mike Shenon. New York: Orchard Books, 1991.

Five mean and hungry boys from a poor area go to their neighbor's house and demand that he make them some food, or else they will steal it. In the end, the neighbor teaches the boys to share and help.

Issues: This story looks at bullying, intimidation, theft, and sharing.

Strategies: Criminal trial based on bullying and intimidation; justice circle.

San Souci, Robert D. Pedro and the Monkey. Illustrated by Robert Hays. New York: Morrow Junior Books, 1996.

This is a Filipino tale about a young farmer who is plagued by a monkey who always steals his corn. One day Pedro captures the monkey – who promptly begs to be set free in exchange for granting Pedro a wish.

Issues: This story looks at theft, contract law, promises, and holding animals captive.

Strategies: Discussion; criminal trial around theft; civil trial regarding contract law; negotiation activity around animal rights.

Van Allsburg, Chris. The Garden of Abdul Gasazi. Illustrated by author. Boston: Houghton Mifflin, 1979

While Alan is taking his neighbor's dog, Fritz, for a walk, Fritz runs off into an eerie-looking garden. This garden belongs to a former magician called Abdul Gasazi, and outside of its gates is a sign that reads "ABSOLUTELY, POSITIVELY, NO DOGS ALLOWED IN THIS GARDEN." Alan must chase Fritz through the garden, where strange things begin to happen.

Issues: This is a story about trespassing and the difference between private and public property.

Strategies: Criminal trial that deals with trespassing, justice circle.

White Deer of Autumn. Ceremony – In the Circle of Life. Illustrated by Daniel San Souci. Milwakee, Wis: Raintree Publishers, 1983.

This is the story of a nine-year-old native American boy called Little Turtle, who is upset by the environmental pollution and destruction in his city. Little Turtle has grown up with no knowledge of his ancestors' beliefs, but he is visited by Star Spirit, who introduces him to traditional teachings and rituals. Through his vision, Little Turtle realizes the knowledge and wisdom of his ancestors.

Issues: This story addresses environmental laws and protection, harmony with nature, and the wisdom of elders.

Strategies: Discussion; mediation activity.

Appendix A: Glossary of Legal Terms

Accused: The person the prosecution claims has broken a criminal law.

Acquit: Declare a person not guilty.

Admissible evidence: Facts, testimony, or objects legally usable to prove a case in court.

Badgering: A lawyer harassing the witness or pestering the witness in a way that is impolite.

Civil law: The area of law involving individuals who have disagreements or disputes with each other (e.g. injuries from a car accident or a conflict over a will). Civil law regulates the laws that are not criminal in nature.

Charge: An accusation brought by the government against someone who has supposedly broken the law. This accusation has not yet been proven in court.

Compromise: The settlement of a dispute by mutual agreement, where both parties give up some demands to reach a settlement.

Concession: The act of giving up a right, privilege, or demand.

Conflict resolution: The process of resolving disputes.

Court: The building or room where a legal case is conducted.

Court artist: The member of the media who is responsible for drawing witnesses and scenes from a trial.

Court clerk: The person who assists the judge in the courtroom by swearing in witnesses and managing the exhibits during the trial.

Court reporter: The person responsible for recording the trial and writing down the times that witnesses begin and end their testimony.

Criminal Code: The Canadian federal statute embodying most of Canada's criminal law and specifying criminal procedures and sentencing options.

Criminal law: The area of law involving charges against individuals for breaking one of the laws of society (e.g. theft or murder). These laws are based on the values we believe in our society, and all citizens should obey these laws. If one of these laws is broken the person is brought to court, tried, and convicted.

Cross-examination: Questions posed to a witness by an opposing lawyer during a trial, following direct examination.

Crown counsel: A lawyer who represents the government and who presents information to try to prove that a crime has been committed and that an accused person has broken a criminal law. Also called the prosecution or prosecutor.

Defense counsel: (defense lawyer) A lawyer who acts on behalf of the accused and presents information to show that either a crime was not committed or the accused person is not guilty of breaking a criminal law.

Defendant: A person who must defend him or herself against a criminal complaint or defend against a civil lawsuit.

Evidence: The information presented by the lawyers and witnesses during a trial.

Exhibit: An object, such as a fingerprint chart, a piece of cloth, or a letter, which is used as evidence by lawyers to prove a case.

Foreperson: The member of a jury who presides over its deliberations and speaks on its behalf.

Guilty beyond a reasonable doubt: The belief that an accused person cannot be found guilty if the judge or the jury has any doubts for which they can give good reasons.

Hearing: A trial. At a hearing all parties listen to the evidence and testimony and make a decision.

Hearsay evidence: Evidence given by a witness based on information received from others rather than personal knowledge. This is not admissible in court.

Indictment: A document containing a charge. Also, a legal process in which a formal accusation is made.

Innocent until proven guilty: The belief that every accused person is not guilty of breaking the law until he or she is proven guilty.

Judge: The pivotal court official who manages the court. The judge listens to evidence, instructs the jury on their role, hears the jury's verdict, and sentences the accused if guilty. In a trial with no jury, the judge decides if a person is guilty or not guilty.

Jury: A group of citizens who find a person guilty or not guilty of breaking the law. In a criminal trial there are 12 jurors and the decision must be unanimous. In a civil trial there are 8 jurors and there must be a majority decision (over 50 percent).

Justice: Conduct done in accordance with what is morally right or fair.

Justice circle: The process in which a group of people in the community gather together to address the effect an offender's crime has had on the victim and the community, agree on a fair and reasonable way for the offender to account for his/her actions, and compensate the victim for the injury.

Law: Rules of conduct determined by legislatures or the courts, intended to maintain order and benefit the public welfare.

Leading questions: A question that prompts the answer wanted.

Liable: Legally responsible.

Libel: a false or misleading publication in writing which tends to harm a person's reputation.

Mediation: The process in which parties involved in a dispute agree to have a neutral person (the mediator) facilitate their discussion and help them reach an agreement.

Mediator: A neutral person who intervenes between parties in a dispute to help them reach an agreement.

Mock trial: A trial that is not a real trial, but a simulated version or role play of a real trial.

Negotiation: The process in which two individuals or parties come together, clarify their problem, identify key issues, and express their opinions about how they think a conflict should be resolved.

Overrule: To reject an objection made by a lawyer in a trial.

Plaintiff: The person or party that brings a lawsuit against another person or party in a civil trial.

Precedent: A previous case or legal decision made by a judge taken as a guide for subsequent cases which are similar in nature.

Prosecution: A lawyer who represents the Crown (the government) and who presents information to try to prove that a crime has been committed and that an accused person has broken a criminal law.

Prosecutor: See prosecution or Crown counsel.

Restorative Justice: The process that brings parties together in a joint solution to meet the needs of everyone involved. It aims to heal the wounds of the victims, offenders, and communities caused by the criminal behavior.

Sentence: The punishment (such as imprisonment or fine) that a judge orders after an accused person is found guilty.

Sheriff: The person who maintains security in the court, protecting the judge and watching over the accused.

Slander: A false oral statement which defames or harms a person's reputation.

Sustain: To uphold or decide in favor of an objection made by a lawyer in a trial.

Testify: To appear as a witness to give evidence under oath in a court of law.

Testimony: Statements made in court by a witness under oath.

Trial: A hearing before a judge, or a judge and jury, to decide if a law has been broken in a criminal trial or to determine if the defendant is liable in a civil trial.

Verdict: The final decision of a judge or jury that a person is guilty or not guilty.

Witness: A person who gives information during the trial.

Appendix B: Legal Organizations and Web Sites

Public Legal Education and Information Organizations

Alberta

Legal Studies Program
University of Alberta
Faculty Extension
University Extension Centre
8303 112th St.
93 University Campus N.W.
Edmonton, Alberta T6G 2T4
Tel: 403-492-5732
www.extension.ualberta.ca/lsp/activ.html

British Columbia

Centre for Education, Law and Society
Simon Fraser University
3230 - 315 West Hastings,
Vancouver, B.C. V6B 5K3
Tel: 604 268-7840
www.educ.sfu.ca/cels

Law Courts Education Society Court House
260-800 Hornby St.
Vancouver, British Columbia
V6Z 2C5
Tel: 604-660-9870
www.lawcourtsed.ca/

Legal Services Society
Suite 1500, 1140 West Pender Street
Vancouver, British Columbia
V6E 4G1
Tel: 604-601-6000
www.lss.bc.ca/

The People's Law School
150-900 Howe Street
Vancouver, BC V6Z 2M4
Tel: 604-331-5400
www.publiclegaled.bc.ca/home/index.htm

Manitoba

Community Legal Education Association
501-294 Portage Ave.
Winnipeg, MB
R3C 0B9
Tel: 204-943-2382
www.acjnet.org/white/clea/

New Brunswick

Public Legal Education and Information
Service of New Brunswick
P.O. Box 6000
Fredericton, New Brunswick E3B 5H1
Tel: 506-453-5369
www.legal-info-legale.nb.ca/

Newfoundland

Public Legal Information of Newfoundland
Suite 101, Fortis Building
139 Water Street
St. John's, NL A1C 1B2
Tel: 709-722-2643
www.publiclegalinfo.com/

Northwest Territories

Law Society of the Northwest Territories
4916-47 Street
P.O. Box 1320
Yellowknife, Northwest Territories
X1A 2L9
Tel: 403-921-2360

Nova Scotia

Legal Education Society of Nova Scotia
911-6080 Young Street
Halifax, Nova Scotia B3K 5L2
Tel: 902-454-2198
www.legalinfo.org/

Ontario

Community Legal Education Ontario
119 Spadina Ave., Suite 600
Toronto, Ontario M5V 2L1
Tel: 416-408-4420
www.cleo.on.ca/english/index.htm

Justice for Children and Youth
Suite 405, 720 Spadina Ave.
Toronto, Ontario
M5S 2T9
Tel: 416-920-1633
www.jfcy.org/

Prince Edward Island

Community Legal Information Association
of Prince Edward island
P.O. Box 1207
1st Floor Sullivan Building
Charlottetown, PEI C1A 7M8
Tel: 902-892-0853
www.plea.org/

Quebec

Barreau du Québec
445 boulevard Saint Laurent, S215
Montreal, QC H2Y 2Y7
Tel: 514-954-3459
www.barreau.qc.ca/infos/courrier.asp

Commission des Services Juridiques
2,Complexe Desjardins
Tour de l'Est, Bureau 1404
Montréal, Québec H5B 1B3
Tel: 514-873-3562
www.csj.qc.ca/

Gouvernement du Québec
Ministere de la Justice
Diretion des Communications
1200 route de l'Eglise, 9th Floor
Sainte-Foy, Québec G1V 4M1
www.justice.gouv.qc.ca/francais/accueil.asp

Saskatchewan

Public Legal Education Association of
Saskatchewan
300-201 21st Street East
Saskatoon, Saskatchewan S7K 0B8
Tel: 306-653-1868
www.plea.org/yas/yashome.htm

Yukon

Yukon Public Legal Education Association
C/o Yukon College Library,
P.O. Box 2799
Whitehorse, Yukon Y1A 5K4
Tel: 867-668-5297
www.yplea.com/

Canadian Law Web Sites Designed for Elementary School Students

Access to Justice Network
Federal Department of Justice and the Legal Resource Centre at the University of Alberta, Edmonton.
Classroom resources and Access to Justice
www.acjnet.org/naresources/classroom.aspx

BC Civil Liberties Association
Citizenship teaching module
www.bccla.org/citizenship

Canada's Schoolnet
Lesson plans and on-line mock trials for elementary students
www.acjnet.org/teacher/

Law Courts Education Society of BC
The Learning Centre
Resources and programs for teachers
www.lawcourtsed.ca

The Centre for Education, Law and Society
Law Connection
Simon Fraser University, Burnaby, BC
Articles and lesson plans for classroom use
www.lawconnection.ca

Public Legal Education Association of Saskatchewan
Elementary school resources related to the law
www.plea.org

United Nations - Cyber School Bus
Global legal issues from children's perspectives
www.un.org/pubs/cyberschoolbus.

Goldilocks and the Three Bears Mock Trial

Her Majesty the Queen v. Goldilocks

By Wanda Cassidy

Recommended for Grades 2 to 3

Case for the Prosecution

That Goldilocks deliberately stole food belonging to the three Bears, and broke a chair belonging to Baby Bear.

Case for the Defence

That Goldilocks ate the Bears' food only because she had been lost in the woods for two days and was extremely hungry and thirsty. That when she found the Bears' house, she did not think Baby Bear would mind her eating his porridge as he had shared food with her before. The Defence disputes the Prosecution's theory that Goldilocks broke Baby Bear's chair, instead stating that it was already broken or that it was broken in some other way.

Trial Roles

Judge (best played by an adult)
Prosecution Lawyers 1, 2, and 3
Defence Lawyers 1, 2, and 3

Prosecution Witnesses:
Corporal Fox
Papa Bear
Mama Bear

Defence Witnesses:
Baby Bear
Goldilocks

Officers of the Court:
Court Clerk
Court Reporter
Sheriffs 1 and 2

Members of the Jury (8, 10, or 12 members), one of whom is appointed Foreperson

Members of the Media:
Print journalists
Television reporters
Court artist

Suggestions for Costumes, Props, and Exhibits

Costumes

Judge	Gown
Prosecution Lawyers	Black gowns
Defence Lawyers	Black gowns
Court Clerk	Black gown

Court Reporter	Black gown
Sheriffs 1 and 2	Brown hats and jackets
Corporal Fox	Fox costume or RCMP uniform (red tunic, brown hat)
Goldilocks	Long blonde hair
Papa Bear	Brown fur costume with face paint, neck tie
Mama Bear	Same as above; also apron/skirt
Baby Bear	Same as above; could also wear a bib and carry a stuffed toy
Court Artist	Smock and beret; could carry paper and coloring pencils
Members of the Media	Name tags or press identification attached to hats or jackets, or worn around the neck; could carry pens, notebooks, and cameras
Members of the Jury	Forest animal costumes (with ears, tails, and face paint) or dressed as other inhabitants of Storybook Village

Props

Indictment Easel to hold fingerprint chart

Exhibits

Exhibit 1:	Porridge bowl
Exhibit 2:	Broken chair
Exhibit 3:	Goldilocks' fingerprint chart
Exhibit 4:	Fingerprints lifted from chair and porridge bowl

Procedure

Entering the Courtroom

1. The teacher welcomes the guests and reviews the intent and format of the trial, and the role of the audience.
2. The Prosecution and Defence lawyers arrive and sit at their tables.
3. The witnesses and media arrive and sit in the area reserved for them.
4. Sheriff 1 enters the courtroom with Goldilocks. He/she seats Goldilocks in the prisoner's box, then sits nearby.
5. The Court Clerk and Court Reporter arrive and take their places.
6. Sheriff 2 calls the court to order, and asks everyone to stand.

7.   The Judge and Jury enter the courtroom, accompanied by Sheriff 2 and take their places. After the Judge and Jury are seated down, the public sits down and the trial is ready to begin.

Trial Procedure

1.   The Court Clerk stands and reads the indictment.
2.   The Prosecution and Defence lawyers introduce themselves to the Judge.
3.   Prosecution makes an opening statement to the Jury, presenting what they intend to prove and listing their witnesses: Corporal Fox, Papa Bear, and Mama Bear.
4.   Prosecution calls Corporal Fox to the stand.
5.   Defence cross-examines Corporal Fox.
6.   Prosecution calls Papa Bear to the stand.
7.   Defence cross-examines Papa Bear.
8.   Prosecution calls Mama Bear to the stand.
9.   Defence cross-examines Mama Bear.
10.   Prosecution rises and says to the Judge that the Prosecution's case is concluded.
11.   Defence makes a short opening statement to the Jury, outlining their defence and listing their witnesses: Baby Bear and Goldilocks.
12.   Defence calls Baby Bear to the stand.
13.   Prosecution cross-examines Baby Bear.
14.   Defence calls Goldilocks to the stand.
15.   Defence says that their case is concluded.
16.   Prosecution cross-examines Goldilocks.
17.   Defence makes a closing statement to the Judge and Jury.
18.   Prosecution makes a closing statement to the Judge and Jury.
19.   The Judge makes a brief statement to the Jury, reviewing the charges and instructs them to go to the Jury room to decide their verdict.
20.   Sheriff 2 says "Order in the court. All rise."
21.   The Judge and the Jury exit the courtroom.
22.   The Jury discusses the trial.
23.   Sheriff 2 says, "Order in the court. All rise."
24.   The Judge and Jury return to the courtroom, accompanied by Sheriff 2.
25.   The Judge asks the Jury for the verdict.
26.   The Foreperson reads out the verdict of guilty or not guilty for each charge. If Goldilocks is found guilty of either charge, the Judge will impose an appropriate sentence. Otherwise, the Judge tells Goldilocks that she is free to go.
27.   The Court Clerk adjourns the court.

Trial Script

Sheriff 2:	Order in the court. All rise.
	(Everyone stands as the Jury and then the Judge enter the courtroom, accompanied by Sheriff 2.)
Court Clerk:	This court is now in session. Mr./Madam Justice ~~~ presiding.
Judge:	You may be seated.
	(All participants sit. Sheriff 1 is seated by Goldilocks; Sheriff 2 sits between the Judge and Jury.)
	Are all parties present?
Prosecution 1:	*(Stands and addresses the Judge)* Yes, My Lord/My Lady. In the case of Her Majesty the Queen against Goldilocks, I am _____, and with me are _____ and _____, acting on behalf of the Prosecution.
	(Each member of the Prosecution stands as he/she is introduced; all sit after introductions are finished.)
Defence 1:	*(Stands and addresses the Judge.)* My Lord/My Lady, I am _____, and with me are _____ and _____, acting on behalf of the accused, Goldilocks.
	(Each member of the Defence stands as he/she is introduced; all sit after introductions are finished.)
Judge:	Thank you.
	(To Court Clerk) Please read the charges.
Court Clerk:	*(Stands)* Will the defendant please rise?
	(Goldilocks and Sheriff 1 stand.)
	(Reading from the indictment) Goldilocks, you stand charged that on or about February 1, 20~~, at Storybook Meadows, in the Province/Territory of ~~~, you did commit a theft of a value not exceeding $5 000 by willfully stealing porridge, the property of the three Bears, contrary to section 334(b) of the *Criminal Code of Canada*. How do you plead?
Goldilocks:	Not guilty, My Lord/My Lady.
Court Clerk:	Goldilocks, you stand charged that on or about February 1, 20~~, at Storybook Meadows, in the Province/Territory of ~~~, you did commit mischief by willfully damaging a chair belonging to Baby Bear, contrary to section 430(1) of *The Criminal Code of Canada*.

	How do you plead?
Goldilocks:	Not guilty, My Lord/My Lady.
Court Clerk:	My Lord/My Lady, the accused pleads not guilty to both charges.
Judge:	Thank you. You may be seated.
	(Those standing now sit down.)
Prosecution 1:	My Lord/My Lady, the Prosecution is ready to begin.
	(Opening statement) My Lord/My Lady, we intend to prove that Goldilocks deliberately stole and ate the Bears' food and broke Baby Bear's chair. To support our case, we will be calling Corporal Fox, Papa Bear, and Mama Bear to the stand. I now wish to call Corporal Fox.
	(Corporal Fox enters the witness stand. Usually, all witnesses remain standing only until they have been sworn in, but Corporal Fox remains standing throughout his/her testimony.)
Court Clerk:	(Approaches the witness stand) Do you swear to tell the truth, the whole truth, and nothing but the truth?
Cpl. Fox:	I do.
Court Clerk:	State your name and address, please.
Cpl. Fox:	My name is Corporal Francis/Frances Fox and I live at 63 Grassy Hole, Storybook Village.
Court Clerk:	Thank you.
	(The Court Clerk returns to his/her seat.)
Prosecution 1:	Corporal Fox, how long have you been a member of the police force?
Cpl. Fox:	I have been a member of the Storybook Village police force since 20~~.
Prosecution 1:	Tell me what happened on February 1st of this year.
Cpl. Fox:	I received a telephone call from Papa Bear who lives in Storybook Meadows. I went to Mr. Bear's address and met him and Mama Bear and Baby Bear. Papa Bear showed me three bowls of porridge and a broken chair. He told me that their beds had also been disturbed, as if someone had slept in them, and that he saw a young girl running away from the house.

Prosecution 1:	Can you describe the condition of the porridge bowls and the chair?
Cpl. Fox:	The porridge in the smallest bowl was almost gone and the chair was broken.
Prosecution 1:	What did you do with that porridge bowl and that chair?
Cpl. Fox:	I put the bowl in a plastic bag and put it and the chair in my car.
Prosecution 1:	Is this the same bowl and the same chair?
	(Brings Exhibits 1 and 2 to Corporal Fox to identify.)
Cpl. Fox:	Yes.
Prosecution 1:	My Lord/My Lady, we submit these items as Exhibits 1 and 2.
	(The Court Clerk labels the plastic bag containing the bowl "Exhibit 1" and the chair "Exhibit 2," then shows them to the Jury before showing them to the Judge.)
	Now Corporal Fox, what did you do after you put the bowl and chair in your car?
Cpl. Fox:	I searched the woods and soon found a little blonde girl asleep under a tree. She looked like the little girl the Bears told me about so I arrested her and took her to the police station.
Prosecution 1:	Do you see the same little girl in the courtroom today?
Cpl. Fox:	Yes. *(He/she points to Goldilocks.)*
Prosecution 1:	Let the record show that Corporal Fox has identified the defendant, Goldilocks, as the girl he found in the woods and arrested.
	Corporal Fox, what did you do when you got to the police station?
Cpl. Fox:	I took Goldilocks' fingerprints. I also took the fingerprints off the porridge bowl and chair.
Prosecution 1:	Are these the fingerprint charts?
	(Shows Exhibits 3 and 4 first to Corporal Fox and then to the Defence.)
Cpl. Fox:	Yes.
Prosecution 1:	My Lord/My Lady, we submit these as Exhibits 3 and 4. Will the Court Clerk please label these.
	(The Court Clerk labels Goldilocks' fingerprint chart as "Exhibit 3," and the lifted fingerprints as "Exhibit 4." He/she then shows the exhibits to the Jury before showing them to the Judge.)

	And were the fingerprints taken from Goldilocks and those on the chair and bowl the same?
Cpl. Fox:	Yes.
Prosecution 1:	Thank you. I have no further questions.
Judge:	Does the Defence wish to cross-examine the witness?
Defence 1:	Thank you, My Lord/My Lady.
	Corporal Fox, was Goldilocks a big girl or a little girl?
Cpl. Fox:	She was about the size of Baby Bear.
Defence 1:	Was she thin or fat?
Cpl. Fox:	She was thin.
Defence 1:	What did she say to you when you found her in the woods?
Cpl. Fox:	She said it was good to have some porridge in her tummy because she had been very hungry.
Defence 1:	What did her clothes look like?
Cpl. Fox:	They were torn and messy.
Defence 1:	Did she say anything to you during the ride down to the police station?
Cpl. Fox:	She was mostly crying and didn't say much except that it was so good to have some food in her tummy. She also asked me to help her find her home because she was lost.
Defence 1:	Thank you. No more questions.
Judge:	You may be excused, Corporal Fox.
	(To Prosecution) You may call your next witness.
	(Corporal Fox returns to his/her seat in the courtroom.)
Prosecution 2:	My Lord/My Lady, I call Papa Bear to the stand.
	(Papa Bear enters the witness stand.)
Court Clerk:	*(Approaches the witness stand)* Do you swear to tell the truth, the whole truth, and nothing but the truth?
Papa Bear:	I do.
Court Clerk:	Please state your name and address.
Papa Bear:	My name is Papa Bear and I live at Honeysuckle Cottage, in Storybook Meadows.

Court Clerk:	Thank you. You may be seated.

(Papa Bear sits down in the witness stand. The Court Clerk returns to his/her seat.)

Prosecution 2:	What happened on the morning of February 1st?
Papa Bear:	Mama Bear, Baby Bear, and I sat down for breakfast but our porridge was too, too hot so we took a short walk in the woods so that our porridge would have time to cool down.
Prosecution 2:	What did you find when you got back to your house?
Papa Bear:	When we sat down for breakfast, I noticed that some porridge had been eaten from my bowl and Mama Bear's bowl. Baby Bear's porridge was almost all gone.

Prosecution 2:	What did you do then?
Papa Bear:	I said, "Somebody has been eating my porridge. I wonder who it is." So I looked around and then noticed that Baby Bear's chair was broken.
Prosecution 2:	Was the chair broken before you left?
Papa Bear:	Oh, no. At least, I don't think so.
Prosecution 2:	What did you do then?
Papa Bear:	We checked all over the house and then went upstairs.
Prosecution 2:	What did you see upstairs?
Papa Bear:	I noticed that somebody had been sleeping in my bed. It was all messy. Then I saw a little blonde haired girl jump out of the window and run away.
Prosecution 2:	Do you see this same little girl in the courtroom today?
Papa Bear:	Yes. *(He points to Goldilocks.)*
Prosecution 2:	What did you do then?
Papa Bear:	I was angry so I phoned the police.
Prosecution 2:	No more questions, thank you.

Judge:	Does the Defence wish to cross-examine?
Defence 2:	Yes, My Lord/My Lady.
	(To Papa Bear) Did you see Goldilocks eat the porridge?
Papa Bear:	No.
Defence 2:	Did you see her break the chair?
Papa Bear:	Well, no, but … she must have …
Defence 2:	Have you met Goldilocks before?
Papa Bear:	No.
Defence 2:	Had you heard of Goldilocks before you saw her that day?
Papa Bear:	Yes. She sometimes plays with my son, Baby Bear.
Defence 2:	Thank you. No more questions.
Judge:	You may step down.
	(To Prosecution) You may call your next witness.
	(Papa Bear returns to his seat in the courtroom.)
Prosecution 3:	I call Mama Bear to the stand.
	(Mama Bear enters the witness stand.)
Court Clerk:	*(Approaches the witness stand)* Do you swear to tell the truth, the whole truth, and nothing but the truth?
Mama Bear:	I do.
Court Clerk:	Please give your name and address.
Mama Bear:	Mama Bear. Honeysuckle Cottage, in Storybook Meadows.
Court Clerk:	Thank you. You may be seated.
	(Mama Bear sits down in the witness stand. The Court Clerk returns to his/her seat.)
Prosecution 3:	Had you or Papa Bear or Baby Bear eaten any porridge before going out on the morning of February 1st?
Mama Bear:	No. We didn't eat any because it was just too hot right then.
Prosecution 3:	Were the beds made that morning?
Mama Bear:	Yes. I saw Papa Bear and Baby Bear do it.
Prosecution 3:	Has Goldilocks ever eaten your food before?

Mama Bear:	Yes. One day a few weeks ago, I made a big picnic lunch for Baby Bear. I watched Baby Bear take the lunch into the woods and when he was about to eat it Goldilocks came along and ate some too.
Prosecution 3:	No further questions.
Judge:	Does the Defence wish to cross-examine the witness?
Defence 3:	Yes, My Lord/My Lady.
	Mama Bear, do you like Goldilocks?
Mama Bear:	I have never met her.
Defence 3:	Has Baby Bear shared part of his lunch with Goldilocks any other time than that one day?
Mama Bear:	Well, I've seen them eat his lunch on maybe three or four occasions.
Defence 3:	Do you leave your door unlocked when you leave the house?
Mama Bear:	Oh, yes.
Defence 3:	Have any other animals or people ever come into your house when you've been away?
Mama Bear:	Well, a couple of times we've had to chase out a badger, a racoon, and a deer.
Defence 3:	Could one of these animals have eaten the food and broken the chair?
Mama Bear:	Oh, no. It's definitely Goldilocks.
Defence 3:	Why do you say so?
Mama Bear:	Because she's always eating Baby Bear's food and I'm tired of having her do that.
Defence 3:	But you didn't actually see Goldilocks eat the porridge or break the chair, did you?
Mama Bear:	Well, no …
Defence 3:	No more questions.
Judge:	Mama Bear, you may step down.
	(Mama Bear returns to her seat in the courtroom.)
Prosecution 1:	We rest our case and have no further witnesses, My Lord/My Lady.
Judge:	*(To Defence)* The Defence may present its case.
Defence 1:	*(Opening statement)* My Lord/My Lady, we wish to show that no direct evidence exists to prove that Goldilocks broke the chair, and although she admits to eating the food, she did it because she was starving and she did not think the Bears would mind. The Defence will call Baby Bear and Goldilocks to the stand. I first call Baby Bear to the stand.
	(Baby Bear enters the witness stand.)

Court Clerk:	*(Approaches the witness stand)* Do you swear to tell the truth, the whole truth, and nothing but the truth?
Baby Bear:	I do.
Court Clerk:	State your name and address, please.
Baby Bear:	My name is Baby Bear and I live in Honeysuckle Cottage, Storybook Meadows.
Court Clerk:	Thank you. You may be seated.
	(Baby Bear sits down in the witness stand. The Court Clerk returns to his/her seat.)
Defence 1:	Baby Bear, how do you know Goldilocks?
Baby Bear:	I met her in the woods a few months ago. Her house isn't too far away. We've played together a number of times before.
Defence 1:	Do you like Goldilocks?
Baby Bear:	Oh, yes. She's quite a bit of fun – sometimes.
Defence 1:	What do you mean sometimes?
Baby Bear:	Well, she's sometimes hungry and sad.
Defence 1:	No further questions, My Lord/My Lady.
Judge:	Does the Prosecution wish to cross-examine the witness?
Prosecution 1:	Yes, My Lord/My Lady.
	Baby Bear, during these times you met Goldilocks, did she ever take any food without asking you?
Baby Bear:	Well, once she took an apple and hid it in her coat. When I asked her why she took it, she said she was sorry, but she took it for her mother, who was hungry too.
Prosecution 1:	Baby Bear, do you know it is wrong to take something that doesn't belong to you?
Baby Bear:	Yes.
Prosecution 1:	Did you give Goldilocks permission to eat your porridge on the morning of February 1st?
Baby Bear:	No.
Prosecution 1:	Was your chair broken before you left that morning?
Baby Bear:	I don't think so, but I hadn't sat on it since the day before.

Prosecution 1:	But didn't you sit on it before you decided the porridge was too hot?
Baby Bear:	Oh, yes, you must be right. I forgot.
Prosecution 1:	No further questions.
Judge:	You may step down, Baby Bear.
	(To Prosecution) You may call your next witness.
	(Baby Bear returns to his seat in the courtroom.)
Defence 2:	My Lord/My Lady, I call Goldilocks to the stand.
	(Goldilocks enters the witness stand.)
Court Clerk:	*(Approaches the witness stand)* Do you swear to tell the truth, the whole truth, and nothing but the truth?
Goldilocks:	I do.
Court Clerk:	Please state your name and address.
Goldilocks:	My name is Goldilocks. I live in Tree House 1 on Park Lane in Storybook Meadows.
Court Clerk:	Thank you. You may be seated.
	(Goldilocks sits down in the witness stand. The Court Clerk returns to his/her seat.)
Defence 2:	Goldilocks, who lives with you in your tree house?
Goldilocks:	My mom.
Defence 2:	Do you have enough food to eat at home?
Goldilocks:	No. Sometimes I am very, very hungry. My mother's job doesn't pay very much, so sometimes we don't have enough money to buy groceries.
Defence 2:	Do you know that it is wrong to steal?
Goldilocks:	Yes, I do. I try to be a good girl.
Defence 2:	Can you describe what you were doing just before Corporal Fox found you and arrested you in Storybook Meadows on February 1st of this year?
Goldilocks:	Well, in the morning the day before, I went into the woods to gather some berries for my mom and me to eat. I went in a new direction though, and I got really, really lost. I was lost for a long, long time and I even slept overnight in a hollowed out tree. The next morning I found a house and I knew it was Baby Bear's house since I had seen it before.

Defence 2:	What did you do then?
Goldilocks:	Well, I went to the door and knocked, but nobody came to the door.
Defence 2:	So, what did you do?
Goldilocks:	The door was open so I went in. I smelled this wonderful porridge. I didn't think that the Bears would mind too much if I had a small taste of it, since Baby Bear had given me a sandwich and an apple before, and I was, oh, so hungry and tired.
Defence 2:	And then what did you do?
Goldilocks:	I tried a bit of porridge from a big bowl, then a bit from a smaller bowl, and when I got to the smallest bowl, I ate up all the porridge.
Defence 2:	Did you leave the house then?
Goldilocks:	No, I didn't, because I was still so tired and I didn't know how long it would take me to find my way home. I thought I'd better sit down since I was so tired. So I sat in a big chair, then a medium-sized chair, but they were both too big. When I tried the smallest chair, it was perfect, except the seat fell out.
Defence 2:	Was it broken before you sat on it?
Goldilocks:	I don't know, it could have been. I was too tired to notice.
Defence 2:	What did you do then?
Goldilocks:	I was so tired and I couldn't sleep on the chair so I went upstairs and tried all the beds till one was oh, so comfy, and I went to sleep.
Defence 2:	What do you remember next?
Goldilocks:	I woke up suddenly when I heard a lot of noise and I got so scared – I leaped up and jumped out the window and ran and ran until I fell down. Then I must have fallen asleep.
Defence 2:	Then what?
Goldilocks:	I woke up to see this police officer looking sternly at me and I started to cry.
Defence 2:	No further questions, My Lord/My Lady.
Judge:	Does the Prosecution wish to cross-examine the witness?

Prosecution 2:	Yes, My Lord/My Lady.
	Goldilocks, if you were as hungry as you say you were, why did you not finish the first bowl of porridge that you started eating?
Goldilocks:	It just was too hot. It burned my tongue.
Prosecution 2:	What about the second bowl?
Goldilocks:	I guess it was too hot too.
Prosecution 2:	If you were as hungry as you say you were, why did you only eat Baby Bear's porridge?
Goldilocks:	I don't know. I don't remember. Maybe it tasted better.
Prosecution 2:	Goldilocks, why didn't you wait for the Bears to come home instead of stealing their food?
Defence 2:	*(Stands)* Objection, My Lord/My Lady. It has not been proven that Goldilocks stole the food.
Judge:	Objection sustained. Please rephrase the question.
Prosecution 2:	Goldilocks, why didn't you wait for the Bears to come home before you ate their food?
Goldilocks:	I felt so hungry and tired.
Prosecution 2:	When you got to the house, why didn't you telephone your mother and tell her that you were safe and ask her to come and get you rather than eat the Bears' food and sit on their chairs and sleep in their beds?
Goldilocks:	We are so poor – we don't have a telephone. I couldn't call my mommy.
Prosecution 2:	Thank you. No further questions.
Judge:	You may step down, Goldilocks.
	(Goldilocks returns to her seat in the courtroom.)
	(To Defence) Do you wish to call any further witnesses?
Defence:	No, My Lord/My Lady. We rest our case.
Judge:	*(To Defence)* Thank you. You may now give your closing statement to the Jury.
Defence:	Thank you, My Lord/My Lady.
	(Closing statement) Ladies and gentleman of the Jury, Goldilocks does admit that she ate the porridge belonging to the three Bears, but it was only out of necessity. She had been wandering lost in the woods since the previous day, had not eaten, and was very hungry - so hungry she felt weak and sick. She knew Baby Bear would have let her eat his porridge if he had been there, because he had shared his food with her before. I ask the Jury to find Goldilocks not guilty of theft because of the defence of necessity.

Concerning the second charge of mischief, there is absolutely no direct evidence to show Goldilocks broke Baby Bear's chair. It could have been one of the Bears, another animal who entered the house, or it could have been broken before that day. Or it might simply have been an accident. Goldilocks must be found not guilty of willful damage.

Judge: *(To Defence)* Thank you.

Is the Prosecution ready to deliver its closing statement to the Jury?

Prosecution 2: Yes, thank you, My Lord/My Lady.

(Closing statement) Ladies and gentlemen of the Jury, Goldilocks admitted to committing a crime: she admitted she ate the Bear family's porridge and she knew she was eating food that was not hers. Even though Baby Bear may have shared his food with Goldilocks in the past, this does not mean that she was welcome to come into their house at any time to help herself to a meal. The Bears had not invited her to eat the food. In fact, they were expecting to eat it themselves after they returned home. Goldilocks' defence of necessity should not apply in this case: we know that she was not as hungry as she says she was because she did not finish the first bowl of porridge or the second bowl. I ask for a guilty verdict to the charge of theft.

Although Goldilocks denies the second charge of mischief, it has not been shown that there was anyone else in the house who could have broken Baby Bear's chair. Papa Bear stated that the chair was not broken before they left that morning. We know that Goldilocks used the chair, and whether she broke it out of carelessness or mischief, it fits with her disrespectful attitude towards other people's property. Can you think of any law-abiding person who would walk into someone else's house, help themselves to their food, and sleep in their beds? Goldilocks must also be found guilty of mischief and wilful damage.

Judge: *(To Prosecution)* Thank you.

(To Jury) As members of the Jury, you will have to make a decision of whether Goldilocks is guilty or not guilty for two charges.

Goldilocks stands charged that she:

"Did commit a theft of a value not exceeding $5 000 by willfully stealing porridge, the property of the three Bears, contrary to section 334(b) of *The Criminal Code of Canada*. "Did commit mischief by wilfully damaging a chair belonging to Baby Bear, contrary to section 430(1) of *The Criminal Code of Canada*.

Think about what the witnesses and lawyers said during the trial. Your job is to carefully weigh the evidence from the both the prosecution and defence and their witnesses and come to a decision. You need to decide which witnesses are more believable and which argument is most plausible. You will then vote on each charge. For this trial, your Jury is only required to reach a majority decision.

You now have 15 minutes to discuss the case. When you return, I will ask your Foreperson your verdict.

Sheriff 2: Order in the court. All rise.

(Everyone stands.)

Court Clerk: Court will now adjourn for 15 minutes.

(The Judge and Jury leave the courtroom, followed by Sheriff 2.)

(When the Judge and Jury are ready to return, approximately 15 minutes later, Sheriff 2 enters the courtroom and calls the court to order.)

Sheriff 2: Order in the court. All rise.

(Everyone stands as the Jury and then the Judge enter the courtroom and are seated.)

Court Clerk: Court is now resumed. Please be seated.

(All participants sit.)

Judge: Mr./Madam Foreperson, have you reached a verdict?

Foreperson: *(Stands)* Yes, My Lord/My Lady.

Court Clerk: *(Stands)* Will the defendant please rise?

(Goldilocks and Sheriff 1 stand.)

Judge: *(To Foreperson)* You may read the verdict.

Foreperson: We find the accused, Goldilocks guilty/not guilty of the charge of theft under $5 000, and guilty/not guilty of the charge of mischief by willful damage.

Judge: Thank you.

(The Judge then passes sentence if Goldilocks is found guilty of any of the charges, or acquits Goldilocks if she is found not guilty of both charges.)

Sheriff 1: *(Standing)* All rise.

(All participants stand.)

Court Clerk: This court is now adjourned.

Three Little Pigs Mock Trial

Her Majesty the Queen v. Sneezy the Wolf

By Heather Gascoigne

Recommended for Grades 2 to 5

Case for the Prosecution

That Sneezy the Wolf deliberately committed three counts of mischief, causing malicious damage to the houses of the First, Second, and Third Little Pigs, and committed one count of breaking and entering with intent when he climbed down the chimney of the Third Little Pig's brick house.

Case for the Defence

That Sneezy the Wolf has been wrongfully charged on all counts. He was simply being neighborly when he visited the homes of the First and Second Little Pigs, but unfortunately, due to a medical condition of hay fever at those times, inadvertently caused damage to their homes. He also did not break and enter the Third Little Pig's house, but was checking to see if the three little pigs were all right when he accidentally fell down the chimney.

Trial Roles

Judge (best played by an adult)

Prosecution Lawyers 1, 2, and 3
  Defence Lawyers 1, 2, and 3

Prosecution Witnesses:
  Arresting Officer
  First Little Pig
  Second Little Pig
  Third Little Pig

Defence Witnesses:
  Sneezy the Wolf
  Granny Wolf
  Gingerbread Man

Officers of the Court:
  Court Clerk
  Court Reporter
  Sheriffs 1 and 2

Members of the Jury, one of whom is appointed Foreperson

Members of the Media:
  Print journalists
  Television reporters
  Court Artist

Suggestions for Costumes, Props, and Exhibits

Costumes

Judge	Gown
Prosecution Lawyers	Black gowns
Defence Lawyers	Black gowns
Court Clerk	Black gown
Court Reporter	Black gown
Sheriffs 1 and 2	Brown hats and jackets
Arresting Officer	Policeman's uniform: blue shirt and pants, tie, and badge
Sneezy the Wolf	Brown clothes or fur costume, face paint, and wolf ears
Granny Wolf	Same as above; also glasses and a shawl
Gingerbread Man	Brown clothing and face paint
Three Little Pigs	Pig costumes, face paint, noses, and ears
Court Artist	Smock and beret; could carry paper and coloring pencils
Members of the Media	Name tags or press identification attached to hats or jackets, or worn around the neck; could carry pens, notebooks, and camera
Members of the Jury	Carpenters' or house builders' clothing (e.g., plaid shirts, overalls, neckerchiefs or bandanas, tools sticking out of pockets); or forest animal costumes (with ears, tails, and face paint)

Props

Indictment (a sheet of paper on which the charge is written)

Exhibits

Exhibit 1:	Plastic bag containing straw
Exhibit 2:	Picture of Sneezy the Wolf
Exhibit 3:	Plastic bag containing twigs
Exhibit 4:	Paw prints lifted from chimney and fireplace
Exhibit 5:	Large picture/photograph of soup pot with lid

Procedure

Entering the Courtroom

1. The teacher welcomes the guests and reviews the intent and format of the trial, and the role of the audience.
2. The Prosecution and Defence lawyers arrive and sit at their tables.
3. The witnesses and media arrive and sit in the area reserved for them.
4. Sheriff 1 enters the courtroom with Sneezy the Wolf. He/she seats Sneezy in the prisoner's box, then sits nearby.
5. The Court Clerk and Court Reporter arrive and take their places.

6. Sheriff 2 calls the court to order, and asks everyone to stand.

7. The Judge and Jury enter the courtroom, accompanied by Sheriff 2 and take their places. After the Judge and Jury are seated, the public sits down and the trial is ready to begin.

Trial Procedure

1. The Court Clerk stands and reads the indictment.

2. The Prosecution and Defence lawyers introduce themselves to the Judge.

3. Prosecution makes an opening statement to the Jury, presenting what they intend to prove and listing witnesses who will be called to testify: the arresting officer and the three little pigs.

4. Prosecution calls the arresting officer to the stand.

5. Defence cross-examines the arresting officer.

6. Prosecution calls the First and Second Little Pigs to the stand.

7. Defence cross-examines the First and Second Little Pigs.

8. Prosecution calls the Third Little Pig to the stand.

9. Defence cross-examines the Third Little Pig.

10. Prosecution rises and says to the Judge that the Prosecution's case is concluded.

11. Defence makes a short opening statement to the Jury, outlining their defence and listing their witnesses: Sneezy the Wolf, Granny Wolf, and the Gingerbread Man.

12. Defence calls Sneezy the Wolf to the stand.

13. Prosecution cross-examines Sneezy.

14. Defence calls Granny Wolf to the stand.

15. Prosecution cross-examines Granny Wolf.

16. Defence calls the Gingerbread Man to the stand.

17. Prosecution cross-examines the Gingerbread Man.

18. Defence rises and says to the Judge that the Defence case is concluded.

19. Defence makes a closing statement to the Judge and Jury.

20. Prosecution makes a closing statement to the Judge and Jury.

21. The Judge makes a brief statement to the Jury, reviewing the charges and instructs them to decide their verdict.

22. Sheriff 2 says "Order in the court. All rise."

23. The Judge and the Jury exit the courtroom with Sheriff 2.

24. The Jury discusses the trial.

25. Sheriff 2 says "Order in the court. All rise."

24. The Judge and Jury return to the courtroom, accompanied by Sheriff 2.

25. The Judge asks the Jury for the verdict.

26. The Foreperson reads out the verdict of guilty or not guilty for each charge. If Sneezy the Wolf is found guilty of either charge, the Judge will impose an appropriate sentence. Otherwise, the Judge tells Sneezy the Wolf he is free to go.

27. The Court Clerk adjourns the court.

Trial Script

Sheriff 2:	Order in the court. All rise.
	(Everyone stands as the Jury and then the Judge enter the courtroom.)
Court Clerk:	This court is now in session. Mr./Madam Justice _____ presiding.
Judge:	You may be seated.
	(All participants sit. Sheriff 1 is seated by Sneezy the Wolf; Sheriff 2 sits between the Judge and Jury.)
	Are all parties present?
Prosecution 1:	*(Stands and addresses the Judge)* Yes, My Lord/My Lady. In the case of Her Majesty the Queen against Sneezy the Wolf, I am _____, and with me are _____ and _____,acting on behalf of the Prosecution.
	(Each member of the Prosecution stands as he/she is introduced; all sit after introductions are finished.)
Defence 1:	*(Stands and addresses the Judge)* My Lord/My Lady, I am _____, and with me are _____ and _____ acting on behalf of the accused, Sneezy the Wolf.
	(Each member of the Defence stands as he/she is introduced; all sit after introductions are finished.)
Judge:	Thank you.
	(To Court Clerk) Please read the charge.
Court Clerk:	*(Stands)* Will the defendant please rise?
	(Sneezy the Wolf and Sheriff 1 stand.)
	(Reading from the indictment) Sneezy the Wolf, you stand charged that on or about March 3rd, 20~~, at Storybook Village, in the Province/Territory of ~~ you did commit mischief by willfully damaging the First Little Pig's house of straw, contrary to section 430(1) of *The Criminal Code of Canada.* How do you plead?
Sneezy:	Not guilty, My Lord/My Lady.
Court Clerk:	Sneezy the Wolf, you stand charged that on or about March 10th, 20~~, at Storybook Village, in the Province/Territory of ~~~, you did commit mischief by willfully damaging the Second Little Pig's house of twigs, contrary to section 430(1) of *The Criminal Code of Canada.* How do you plead?
Sneezy:	Not guilty, My Lord/My Lady.

Court Clerk:	Sneezy the Wolf, you stand charged that on or about March 21st, 20~~, at Storybook Village, in the Province/Territory of ~~~, you did commit mischief by willfully attempting to damage the Third Little Pig's house of brick, contrary to section 430(1) of *The Criminal Code of Canada*. How do you plead?
Sneezy:	Not guilty, My Lord/My Lady.
Court Clerk:	Sneezy the Wolf, you stand charged that on or about March 21st, 20~~, at Storybook Village, in the Province/Territory of ~~~, you did commit break and enter of the Third Little Pig's house of brick, with intent to commit an indictable offence therein, contrary to section 348(1)(a) of *The Criminal Code of Canada*. How do you plead?
Sneezy:	Not guilty, My Lord/My Lady.
Court Clerk:	My Lord/My Lady, the accused pleads not guilty to all charges.
Judge:	Thank you. You may be seated.
	(Those standing now sit down.)
	Prosecution, please proceed with your case.
Prosecution 1:	*(Opening statement)* My Lord/My Lady, we intend to show that Sneezy the Wolf deliberately created mischief, and caused malicious damage to the houses of the First and Second Little Pigs by huffing and puffing and blowing them down. We also intend to prove that he did break and enter when he climbed down the chimney of the Third Little Pig's house.
	To support our case, we will be calling the Arresting Officer and the Three Little Pigs as witnesses. We now wish to call the Arresting Officer to the stand.
	(The Arresting Officer enters the witness stand. Usually, all witnesses remain standing only until they have been sworn in, but the Arresting Officer remains standing throughout his/her testimony.)
Court Clerk:	*(Approaches the witness stand)* Do you swear to tell the truth, the whole truth, and nothing but the truth?
Arresting Officer:	I do.
Court Clerk:	State your name and address, please.
Arresting Officer:	I am the Arresting Officer, and I live in Storybook Village.
Court Clerk:	Thank you.
	(The Court Clerk returns to his/her seat.)

Prosecution 1:	Officer, do you know Storybook Village well?
Arresting Officer:	Yes, I have lived there for many years and know all the residents of Storybook Village very well.
Prosecution 1:	Please tell the court what happened on the morning of March 3rd, 20~~.
Arresting Officer:	I received a call to proceed to the vicinity of the First Little Pig's house.
Prosecution 1:	What did you find when you got there?
Arresting Officer:	Nothing but a pile of straw, and a Little Pig who appeared to be very upset.
Prosecution 1:	Did you take any evidence at the scene of the crime?
Arresting Officer:	Yes. Here is a sample of the straw.
	(He/she holds up a plastic bag containing straw.)
Prosecution 1:	Thank you. My Lord/My Lady, we submit this as Exhibit 1.
	(The Court Clerk labels the plastic bag "Exhibit 1," then shows it to the Jury before showing it to the Judge.)
Prosecution 1:	Now, Officer, what did you do next?
Arresting Officer:	I questioned the witness *(points to the First Little Pig)* and asked him to come down to the station to look at some photos, to see if he could make a positive identification.
Prosecution 1:	And was he able to?
Arresting Officer:	Yes … he identified this one!
	(He/she holds up a picture of Sneezy.)
Prosecution 1:	Whose picture is this?
Arresting Officer:	Sneezy the Wolf.
Prosecution 1:	Thank you. I wish to submit this picture as Exhibit 2.
	(The Court Clerk labels the picture "Exhibit 2," then shows it to the Jury before showing it to the Judge.)
Prosecution 1:	Officer, what did you do next?
Arresting Officer:	I took the First Little Pig over to his brother's house of bricks.
Prosecution 1:	Thank you. Now Officer, please tell us what happened on the 10th day of March, 20~~.
Arresting Officer:	I received a call requesting me to proceed to a disturbance in the vicinity of the Second Little Pig's house of twigs.
Prosecution 1:	And what did you find this time?

Arresting Officer:	Nothing but a pile of twigs, and a Little Pig who appeared to be very angry.
Prosecution 1:	Did you take any evidence at the scene of the crime?
Arresting Officer:	Yes.
	(He/she holds up a plastic bag with twigs inside.)
Prosecution 1:	Thank you. My Lord/My Lady, we would like to submit this as Exhibit 3.
	(The Court Clerk labels the plastic bag "Exhibit 3," then shows it to the Jury before showing it to the Judge.)
	Now Officer, what did you do next?
Arresting Officer:	I questioned the Second Little Pig, then took him down to the station to give a statement.
Prosecution 1:	And what happened on the 21st day of March, 20~~?
Arresting Officer:	I was called to the home of the Third Little Pig.
Prosecution 1:	What did you find when you got there?
Arresting Officer:	All Three Little Pigs were there and appeared to be jumping up and down with excitement. They said they had caught Sneezy inside a big soup pot in the fireplace and had slammed the lid down.
Prosecution 1:	Did you take any evidence?
Arresting Officer:	Yes. I took samples of paw prints from around the top of the chimney and down the inside of the fireplace and also prints from the accused.
	(He/she holds up paw print chart.)
Prosecution 1:	Do the paw prints from the chimney and the fireplace match those of anyone in the courtroom today?
Arresting Officer:	Yes! Sneezy the Wolf!
	(He/she hands the chart to the Court Clerk.)
Prosecution 1:	My Lord/My Lady, we submit these paw prints as Exhibit 4.
	(The Court Clerk labels the chart "Exhibit 4," then shows it to the Jury before showing it to the Judge.)
	Thank you. No further questions.
Judge:	Does the Defence wish to cross-examine?
Defence 1:	Thank you, My Lord/My Lady.
	Officer, isn't it true that March 3rd was a very windy day?

Arresting Officer:	Well … yes … I remember it was more windy than usual.
Defence 1:	And isn't it possible that the First Little Pig's poorly built house of straw could have been blown down by the wind on such a blustery day?
Prosecution 1:	My Lord/My Lady, I object! This calls for a conclusion on the part of the witness.
Judge:	Objection sustained.
Defence 1:	Sorry, My Lord/My Lady. Well then, was it windy enough to blow the branches of the trees?
Arresting Officer:	Yes, the branches were moving
Defence 1:	Thank you. No further questions.
Judge:	*(To Arresting Officer)* You may step down.
	(To Prosecution) You may call your next witness.
	(The Arresting Officer returns to his/her seat in the courtroom.)
Prosecution 2:	We call the First and Second Little Pigs to the stand, My Lord/My Lady.
	(The First and Second Little Pigs enter the witness stand.)
Court Clerk:	*(Approaches the witness stand)* Do you swear to tell the truth, the whole truth, and nothing but the truth?
First & Second Little Pigs: We do. *(in unison)*	
Court Clerk:	State your names and addresses, please.
First Little Pig:	I am the First Little Pig.
Second Little Pig:	I am the Second Little Pig.
First & Second Little Pigs:	We now live with our brother/sister in his/her house at 1 Red Brick Lane, in Storybook Village.
Court Clerk:	Thank you. You may be seated.
	(The First and Second Little Pigs sit down together in the witness stand. The Court Clerk returns to his/her seat.)
Prosecution 2:	First Little Pig, tell the court what happened on March 3rd, 20~~.
First Little Pig:	I looked out my window and saw that wolf!
	(He/she points to Sneezy.)
Prosecution 2:	*(To Judge)* Let the record show that the witness has identified the accused.
	(To First Little Pig) And then what happened?

First Little Pig:	He said, "Little Pig, Little Pig, let me in … or I'll huff and I'll puff and I'll blow your house down!"
Prosecution 2:	And what happened?
First Little Pig:	All of a sudden I felt a big gust of air, and my house of straw was completely blown away! I was so frightened I squealed and ran to my brother's house.
Prosecution 2:	Second Little Pig, please tell the court what happened on March 10th, 20~~.
Second Little Pig:	I was at home, reading a book, and suddenly I heard a voice outside saying, "Little Pig, Little Pig, let me in … or I'll huff and I'll puff and I'll blow your house down!"
Prosecution 2:	And what happened?
Second Little Pig:	All of a sudden I felt a big gust of air, and my house of twigs came tumbling down around me!
Prosecution 2:	Did you see anyone?
Second Little Pig:	Yes! I was squealing very loudly and scared him away, but I saw a wolf running into the woods!
Prosecution 2:	Did you see anyone else?
Second Little Pig:	Yes, I thought I saw a gingerbread man running over the hill.
Prosecution 2:	Thank you. No further questions.
Judge:	Does the Defence wish to cross-examine?
Defence 2:	Yes, My Lord/My Lady.
	First Little Pig, how could you possibly expect your house to last when you built it out of straw? You must have known that a strong wind could bring it down.
First Little Pig:	But it wasn't the wind!
Defence 2:	And, Second Little Pig, how do you know it was a wolf outside your house of twigs? Didn't you also just say that you thought you saw a gingerbread man running over the hill?
Second Little Pig:	Well … yes … but …
Defence 2:	Thank you. No further questions, My Lord/My Lady.
Judge:	(*To First and Second Little Pigs*) You may step down.
	(*The First and Second Little Pigs return to their seats in the courtroom.*)

	(To Prosecution) Do you wish to call any further witnesses?
Prosecution 3:	Yes, My Lord/My Lady. We call the Third Little Pig to the stand.
	(The Third Little Pig enters the witness stand.)
Court Clerk:	*(Approaches the witness stand)* Do you swear to tell the truth, the whole truth, and nothing but the truth?
Third Little Pig:	I do.
Court Clerk:	State your name and address, please.
Third Little Pig:	I am the Third Little Pig, and I live in my house at 1 Red Brick Lane.
Court Clerk:	Thank you. You may be seated.
	(The Third Little Pig sits down in the witness stand. The Court Clerk returns to his/her seat.)
Prosecution 3:	Third Little Pig, please tell the court what happened on March 21st, 20~~.
Third Little Pig:	I heard a knock on my front door, and when I peeked out the window, I saw a wolf!
Prosecution 3:	Do you see that wolf in the courtroom today?
Third Little Pig:	Yes! *(Points to Sneezy.)*
Prosecution 3:	*(To Judge)* May the records show that the witness has identified the accused. Now, Third Little Pig, did you hear anything after the knock on your door?
Third Little Pig:	Yes, the wolf was shouting, "Little Pig, Little Pig, let me in, or I'll huff and I'll puff and I'll blow your house down!"
Prosecution 3:	Did you answer?
Third Little Pig:	No. I heard him huffing and puffing, but I'd built my house of brick and I knew he couldn't blow it down.
Prosecution 3:	What happened next?
Third Little Pig:	I heard him climbing up onto the roof and crawling towards the chimney.
Prosecution 3:	Is that when you phoned the police and told them it was the wolf and that he was going to eat you?
Defence 3:	My Lord/My Lady, I object – leading the witness!
Judge:	Objection sustained. Ask the question a different way.
Prosecution 3:	I will rephrase my question. Third Little Pig, what did you do then?

Third Little Pig:	I called my two brothers/sisters to help me – they've been staying with me since their houses were destroyed.
Prosecution 3:	What did the three of you do?
Third Little Pig:	Well, First and Second Little Pigs pulled the big soup pot into the fireplace, and when the wolf fell down the chimney into the pot, I slammed the lid down tight. Then we called the police.
Prosecution 3:	Thank you. No further questions, My Lord/My Lady.
Judge:	Does the Defence wish to cross-examine?
Defence 3:	Yes, My Lord/My Lady.
	Third Little Pig, your house is made of brick?
Third Little Pig:	Yes.
Defence 3:	The doors were locked?
Third Little Pig:	Yes.
Defence 3:	The windows were closed?
Third Little Pig:	Yes.
Defence 3:	And yet you say you could clearly hear the wolf?
Third Little Pig:	I thought I could.
Defence 3:	No further questions, My Lord/My Lady.
Judge:	*(To Third Little Pig)* You may step down.
	(The Third Little Pig returns to his/her seat in the courtroom.)
	Does the Prosecution wish to call any further witnesses?
Prosecution 3:	No, My Lord/My Lady. We rest our case.
Judge:	*(To Prosecution)* Thank you.
	(To Defence) The Defence may begin.
Defence 1:	*(Opening statement)* My Lord/My Lady, we intend to show that Sneezy the Wolf has been wrongfully charged on all counts. Our client is known as Sneezy because he suffers greatly from hay fever every spring. It was spring when these charges were laid, and Sneezy's medical condition at the time has resulted in his good intentions being misinterpreted. He had no intention of causing harm to the Three Little Pigs – he was simply making friendly visits to his three closest neighbors when overcome by hay fever attacks.
	To support our case, we will be calling Sneezy himself, Granny Wolf, and the Gingerbread Man as witnesses.
	We now call Sneezy to the stand.

(Sneezy the Wolf enters the witness stand. Sheriff 1 follows Sneezy to the witness box and stands nearby.)

Court Clerk:	*(Approaches the witness stand)* Do you swear to tell the truth, the whole truth, and nothing but the truth?
Sneezy:	I do.
Court Clerk:	State your name and address, please.
Sneezy:	My name is Sneezy the Wolf, and I live in the woods outside Storybook Village.
Court Clerk:	Thank you. You may be seated.

(Sneezy sits down in the witness stand. The Court Clerk returns to his/her seat.)

Defence 1:	Sneezy, how did you get your nickname?
Sneezy:	Every spring, I suffer from very bad hay fever.
Defence 1:	I see. Now, can you tell the court what you were doing on March 3rd, 20~~?
Sneezy:	Well, it was one of those early spring days, sunny and cool, but quite windy. I decided to pay a neighborly visit to the First Little Pig who lived just down the road.
Defence 1:	I see. Had you ever visited him before?
Sneezy:	No. Actually, he and his brothers had just recently moved into the area, and I thought it would be a friendly thing to do – to go along and welcome them to the neighborhood.
Defence 1:	And what happened when you got to the First Little Pig's house?
Sneezy:	Well, I was standing back and admiring the nice job he'd made of building a house out of straw, when all of a sudden, there was a strong gust of wind that blew some dust and pollen up my nose, and I sneezed!
Defence 1:	And what happened to the house of straw?
Sneezy:	It fell apart!
Defence 1:	Did you say you'd huff and you'd puff and blow his house down?
Sneezy:	Oh no! I did say to myself "Oh dear, I'm huffing and puffing and need to blow my nose." And then I sneezed.
Defence 1:	And on March 10th, did something very similar happen?

Sneezy:	Yes. I decided to go along to the Second Little Pig's house to tell him how sorry I was about what happened to his brother's house.
Defence 1:	And when you got there?
Sneezy:	Well, I had just opened up my mouth to call out, "Yoohoo… anybody home?" when I sneezed again and his house of twigs fell apart.
Defence 1:	What did you do?
Sneezy:	Well, I remembered how angry the First Little Pig had been, so I ran off into the woods.
Defence 1:	Had you meant to do any harm?
Sneezy:	No! Absolutely not!
Defence 1:	And on March 21st, 20~~ did you try to break into the Third Little Pig's house of brick, by climbing down his chimney?
Sneezy:	No! I knew all three Little Pigs were living there together, and went over to offer my assistance in helping the First and Second Little Pigs rebuild their homes.
Defence 1:	What happened this time?
Sneezy:	I very politely knocked on the front door and asked if they were in.
Defence 1:	Did they answer?
Sneezy:	Well, I couldn't tell … I heard a sound, like something was being dragged across the floor, and I was worried that maybe something was wrong inside.
Defence 1:	What did you do?
Sneezy:	Well, the doors were all locked, and the curtains shut, so I decided to jump onto the roof and see if I could look down the chimney to make sure they were okay.
Defence 1:	What happened when you looked down the chimney?

Sneezy:	Just as I was peering down, some smoke got up my nose, and I gave a terrific sneeze and lost my balance, and fell down the chimney!
Defence 1:	Did the Three Little Pigs come to your rescue?
Sneezy:	No! Definitely not! I'd fallen into a pot, and they clamped the lid on tight and kept me there until a police officer arrived. I thought it was very ungracious of them!

Defence 1:	*(Holding a picture/photograph towards Sneezy)* Sneezy, please look at this picture/photograph carefully. Is this the pot in which the Three Little Pigs had you trapped?
Sneezy:	Yes! That's it! It was most uncomfortable!
Defence 1:	My Lord/My Lady, we would like to submit this picture/photograph as Exhibit 5.

(He/she hands the picture/photograph to the Court Clerk.)

(The Court Clerk labels the picture/photograph "Exhibit 5," then shows it to the Jury, before showing it to the Judge.)

Thank you, Sneezy. No further questions.

Judge:	Does the Prosecution wish to cross-examine?
Prosecution 1:	Yes, My Lord/My Lady.
	Sneezy, you were present both when the First Little Pig's house of straw collapsed and when the Second Little Pig's house of twigs had fallen in?
Sneezy:	It was just coincidence. It wasn't my fault – I was just trying to be neigh-borly.

Prosecution 1:	And do you really expect us to believe this story about your hay fever when you haven't sneezed once in this courtroom today?
Sneezy:	Well, um … I guess it's not very dusty in here. This place isn't made of straw or twigs!
Prosecution 1:	You heard the evidence of the Three Little Pigs that you said you'd huff and you'd puff and you'd blow their house in?

Sneezy:	I think what they heard was me talking to myself and then my sneezing.
Prosecution 1:	Do you mean that to say that it was only a coincidence that each of the Little Pigs heard you make that statement, on each of the three separate occasions that you visited them, just before their house was destroyed?
Sneezy:	Um, I guess, yeah.
Prosecution 1:	No further questions, My Lord/My Lady.
Judge:	*(To Sneezy)* You may step down.
	(Sneezy returns to his seat in the courtroom.)
	Will the Defence please call their next witness.
Defence 2:	We call Granny Wolf to the stand.
	(Granny Wolf enters the witness stand.)
Court Clerk:	*(Approaches the witness stand)* Do you swear to tell the truth, the whole truth and nothing but the truth?
Granny Wolf:	I do.
Court Clerk:	State your name and address, please.
Granny Wolf:	Granny Wolf, and I live in a little cottage in the woods, just down the lane from Little Red Riding Hood.
Court Clerk:	Thank you. You may be seated.
	(Granny Wolf sits down in the witness stand. The Court Clerk returns to his/her seat.)
Defence 2:	Now, Granny, have you known Sneezy for long?
Granny Wolf:	Yes, we've known each other for years.
Defence 2:	Does Sneezy have a reputation for huffing and puffing?
Prosecution 2:	My Lord/My Lady, I object. What does "reputation" mean? Is she an expert?
Judge:	Objection sustained, but please rephrase the question leaving out the word reputation.
Defence 2:	*(To Judge)* Yes, my Lord/My Lady.
	(To Granny Wolf) Would you say Sneezy huffs and puffs in your presence?
Granny Wolf:	Why, yes. In the spring his voice is raspy and he is often short of breath.
Defence 2:	Did you know that Sneezy suffers from hay fever?
Granny Wolf:	Oh yes. It's well known that he's very allergic to all sorts of pollen, as well as straw, dust, and smoke. That's why we call him Sneezy.

Defence 2:	Did you know that Sneezy was going to visit the Three Little Pigs?
Granny Wolf:	Yes. He told me he was going to pay them a visit to welcome them to our neighborhood.
Defence 2:	Thank you, Granny. No further questions, My Lord/My Lady.
Judge:	Does the Prosecution wish to cross-examine?
Prosecution 2:	Yes, My Lord/My Lady. Granny, why did you not go along with Sneezy to welcome the Three Little Pigs to the neighborhood?
Granny Wolf:	Well, I'm not as young as I used to be …
Prosecution 2:	Has Sneezy ever sneezed hard enough to damage your house?
Granny Wolf:	No, I can't say that he has, but his sneezes have seemed to be getting worse lately.
Prosecution 2:	Seeing that you are such good friends, have you ever tried to help Sneezy get over these hay fever attacks?
Granny Wolf:	Oh, Sneezy can take care of himself well enough without my help. It's not as if it's a life and death situation – well, you know what I mean…
Prosecution 2:	And Granny, I find it rather unusual that my learned colleagues for the Defence would call on you as a character witness for the accused. Why, aren't you the one who was suspected of eating Little Red Riding Hood's Grandmother?
Defence 2:	My Lord/My Lady, I object! This is a different story! Granny is not the accused in this trial!
Judge:	Objection sustained. This comment is inappropriate and you don't need to answer this, Granny.
Prosecution 2:	Sorry, My Lord/My Lady. No further questions.
Judge:	*(To Granny Wolf)* You may step down. *(Granny Wolf returns to her seat in the courtroom.)* Does the Defence wish to call any further witnesses?
Defence 2:	Yes, My Lord/My Lady. We call the Gingerbread Man to the stand. *(The Gingerbread Man enters the witness stand.)*
Court Clerk:	*(Approaches the witness stand)* Do you swear to tell the truth, the whole truth, and nothing but the truth?

Gingerbread Man:	I do.
Court Clerk:	State your name and address, please.
Gingerbread Man:	I am the Gingerbread Man, and I lived for a very short while at Candy Farm in Storybook Village. I'm presently looking for a new place to live.
Court Clerk:	Thank you. You may be seated.

(The Gingerbread Man sits down in the witness stand. The Court Clerk returns to his/her seat.)

Defence 3:	Now, Gingerbread Man, please tell the court what happened on March 10th, 20~~.
Gingerbread Man:	Well, I'd just come out of the oven after a dear little woman had baked me, and when she took me out of the oven and put me on the windowsill to cool, I jumped up and ran as fast as I could.
Defence 3:	Where were you going?
Gingerbread Man:	Anywhere … I was just having fun!
Defence 3:	Were you chased by anyone?
Gingerbread Man:	Yes, but they weren't very fast, so as I ran I yelled, "Run, run, as fast as you can. You can't catch me I'm the Gingerbread Man!"
Defence 3:	Where did you run to?
Gingerbread Man:	Through the village and down the lane towards the woods.
Defence 3:	Did you go past the Second Little Pig's house of twigs?
Gingerbread Man:	Yes … and then over the hill.
Defence 3:	Did you see or hear anything as you ran past?
Gingerbread Man:	Well, I saw the wolf called Sneezy and just as I ran past, he gave a great big sneeze, and the house of twigs came tumbling down.
Defence 3:	Did you hear him threaten anyone?
Gingerbread Man:	No, in fact as I ran past, I was shouting, "Run, run as fast as you can. You can't catch me, I'm the Gingerbread Man!"
Defence 3:	Do you think that's what the Second Little Pig actually heard?
Prosecution 3:	Objection! This calls for a supposition on the part of the witness. He can't be expected to know what the Second Little Pig thought he heard.
Judge:	Objection sustained. Defence, your questions called for hearsay. Please rephrase your question.
Defence 3:	Gingerbread Man, were you shouting loud enough that someone inside the house of twigs could hear you?
Gingerbread Man:	Maybe. Anyway, as I ran over the hill, I saw the wolf scamper off into the woods.

Defence 3:	Thank you. No further questions.
Judge:	Does the Prosecution wish to cross-examine?
Prosecution 3:	Yes, My Lady/My Lord.
	Gingerbread Man, it doesn't seem very polite for you to run away like that?
Gingerbread Man:	Well, no, but I was just having some fun.
Prosecution 3:	Were you running very fast?
Gingerbread Man:	Oh yes! No one could catch me! They ran and ran as fast as they could, but they couldn't catch me, I'm …
Prosecution 3:	*(Interrupts)* Yes, yes, we know. But if you were running past the Second Little Pig's twig house so fast, how can you be sure exactly what you saw and heard?
Gingerbread Man:	Well, um …
Prosecution 3:	Thank you. No further questions, My Lord/My Lady.
Judge:	*(To Gingerbread Man)* You may step down.
	(The Gingerbread Man returns to his courtroom seat.)
Defence 3:	We rest our case, My Lord/My Lady.
Judge:	*(To Defence)* Thank you. You may now give your closing statement to the Jury.
Defence 3:	Thank you, My Lord/My Lady.

(Closing statement) Ladies and gentlemen of the Jury, we have shown that poor Sneezy the Wolf has been unjustly accused of these crimes. His only intention was to be friendly and helpful. Sneezy was the only inhabitant of Storybook Village to make a special effort to visit the Three Little Pigs to welcome them to the neighborhood. He should not be blamed for having hay fever. He had no intention to sneeze down the First and Second Little Pigs' houses. It was not willful destruction. Consider how poorly built these two houses were.

We have established that on March 21st, Sneezy did not intentionally break and enter the Third Little Pig's house of brick. I remind you that he was concerned with the welfare of the Three Little Pigs when they did not answer the door. In trying to check that they were safe and had not had an accident in their new house, poor

remem-
inside
all
charges.

Sneezy accidentally sneezed and fell down the chimney. Please remember how badly treated he was by all Three Pigs who trapped him inside a pot! We are sure that you will find Sneezy not guilty of all charges. Thank you.

Judge: *(To Defence)* Thank you.

(To Prosecution) Would you please give your closing statement to the Jury.

Prosecution 3: Thank you, My Lord/My Lady.

(Closing statement) Ladies and gentlemen of the Jury, there can be no doubt that Sneezy deliberately caused malicious damage to the property of the First and Second Little Pigs. Section 430(1) of *The Criminal Code of Canada* states that "everyone commits mischief who wilfully destroys or damages property . . . and renders that property useless . . ." What would state more clearly the effect Sneezy had on the house of straw, and the house of twigs? He did it on purpose.

We also contend that he deliberately climbed down the chimney of the Third Little Pig's house of brick. That was no accident! It is impossible to believe that Sneezy was only trying to be neighborly. Every time he visited one of the Three Little Pigs, disaster struck! If he was that worried, why did he knock on the door? We remind you that the definition of breaking and entering includes entering a place by threat or trick, with intent to commit a crime.

We ask that you find Sneezy the Wolf guilty of all charges. Thank you.

Judge: *(To Prosecution)* Thank you.

(To Jury) As members of the Jury, you will have to make a decision of whether Sneezy the Wolf is guilty or not guilty for each charge.

Sneezy the wolf stands charged that he:

"Did commit mischief by willfully damaging the First Little Pig's house of straw, contrary to section 430(1) of *The Criminal Code of Canada*.

"Did commit mischief by willfully damaging the Second Little Pig's house of twigs, contrary to section 430(1) of *The Criminal Code of Canada*.

"Did commit mischief by willfully attempting to damage the Third Little Pig's house of brick, contrary to section 430(1) of *The Criminal Code of Canada*.

"Did break and enter the Third Little Pig's house of brick, with intent to commit an indictable offence therein, contrary to section 348(1)(a) of *The Criminal Code of Canada.*"

Think about what the witnesses and lawyers said during the trial. Your job is to carefully weigh the evidence from the both the prosecution and defence and their witnesses and come to a decision. You need to decide which witnesses are more believable and which argument is most plausible. You will then vote on each charge. For this trial, your Jury is only required to reach a majority decision.

You now have 15 minutes to discuss the case. When you return, I will ask your Foreperson your verdict.

Sheriff 2:	Order in the court. All rise.
	(Everyone stands.)
Court Clerk:	Court will now adjourn for 15 minutes.
	(The Judge and Jury leave the courtroom, followed by Sheriff 2.)
	(When the Judge and Jury are ready to return, approximately 15 minutes later, Sheriff 2 enters the courtroom and calls the court to order.)
Sheriff 2:	Order in the court. All rise.
	(Everyone stands as the Jury and then the Judge enter the courtroom and are seated.)
Court Clerk:	Court is now resumed. Please be seated.
	(All other participants sit.)
Judge:	Mr./Madam Foreperson, have you reached a verdict?
Foreperson:	*(Stands)* Yes, My Lord/My Lady.
Court Clerk:	*(Stands)* Will the defendant please rise?
	(Sneezy and Sheriff 1 stand.)
Judge:	*(To Foreperson)* You may read the verdict.
	Foreperson: We find the accused, Sneezy the Wolf, guilty/not guilty of the charge of mischief to the First Little Pig's house of straw, guilty/not guilty of the charge of mischief to the Second Little Pig's house of twigs, guilty/not guilty of the charge of mischief to the Third Little Pig's house of bricks, and guilty/not guilty of the charge of breaking and entering the Third Little Pig's house of brick.
Judge:	Thank you.
	(The Judge then passes sentence if Sneezy is found guilty of any of the charges, or acquits Sneezy if he is found not guilty of all charges.)
Sheriff 1:	*(Standing)* Order in the court. All rise.
	(All participants stand.)
Court Clerk:	This court is now adjourned.

Peter Pan Mock Trial

Her Majesty the Queen v. Peter Pan

By Heather Gascoigne

Recommended for Grades 3 to 4

Case for the Prosecution

That Peter Pan should be found guilty of abduction of three persons under 14 years, namely Wendy, John, and Michael Darling, from their parents, Mr. and Mrs. George Darling, and their nurse dog, Nana.

Case for the Defence

That Peter did not come to the Darlings' home with the intent to cause trouble. The night he entered the nursery, he and Tinker Bell were looking for his lost shadow and accidentally woke the children. While Wendy sewed his shadow back on for him, the children asked to be taken to Neverland and flew off with Peter willingly. Therefore Peter did not deliberately intend to deprive their parents and their nurse of the possession of the children. The children had chosen to visit Neverland and it was always Peter's intention to return them to their home eventually.

Trial Roles

Judge (best played by an adult)

Prosecution Lawyers 1, 2, and 3
Defence Lawyers 1, 2, and 3

Prosecution Witnesses:
Arresting Officer
Nana
Captain Hook

Defence Witnesses:
Peter Pan
Wendy Darling
Tinker Bell

Officers of the Court:
Court Clerk
Court Reporter
Sheriffs 1 and 2
Members of the Jury, one of whom is appointed Foreperson

Members of the Media
Print journalists
Television reporters
Court Artist

Suggestions for Costumes, Props, and Exhibits

Costumes

Judge	Gown
Prosecution Lawyers	Black gowns
Defence Lawyers	Black gowns

Court Clerk	Black gown
Court Reporter	Black gown
Sheriffs 1 and 2	Brown hats and jackets
Arresting Officer	Policeman's uniform: blue shirt and pants, tie, and badge
Nana (a Newfoundland dog)	Dog costume, floppy ears
Captain Hook	Pirate costume, shirt with ruffles, a hook for the right hand
Peter Pan	Tights, tunic made of leaves
Wendy Darling	Nightgown and slippers
Tinker Bell	Fairy costume or tights and tunic also
Court Artist	Smock and beret; could carry paper and coloring pencils
Members of the Media	Name tags or press identification attached to hats or jackets, or worn around the neck; could carry pens, notebooks, and cameras
Members of the Jury	Children who are about to be tucked into bed: pyjamas, dressing gowns, carrying teddy bears.

Props

Indictment (a sheet of paper on which the charge is written)

Exhibits

Exhibit 1:	Finger print chart
Exhibit 2:	Plastic bag containing fairy dust (glittery powder)
Exhibit 3:	Peter Pan's shadow

Procedure

Entering the Courtroom

1. The teacher welcomes the guests and reviews the intent and format of the trial, and the role of the audience.
2. The Prosecution and Defence Lawyers arrive and sit at their tables.
3. The witnesses and media arrive and sit in the areas reserved for them.
4. Sheriff 1 enters the courtroom with Peter. He/she seats Peter in the prisoner's box and then sits nearby.
5. The Court Clerk and Court Reporter arrive and take their places.
6. Sheriff 2 calls the court to order, and asks everyone to stand.
7. The Judge and Jury enter the courtroom with Sheriff 2 and take their places. After the Judge is seated, the public sits down and the trial is ready to begin.

Trial Procedure

1. The Court Clerk stands and reads out the indictment.
2. The Prosecution and Defence lawyers introduce themselves to the Judge.
3. Prosecution makes an opening statement to the Jury, presenting what they intend to prove and listing their witnesses: the arresting officer, Nana, and Captain Hook.
4. Prosecution calls the arresting officer to the stand.
5. Defence cross-examines the arresting officer.
6. Prosecution calls Nana to the stand.
7. Defence cross-examines Nana.
8. Prosecution calls Captain Hook to the stand.
9. Defence cross-examines Captain Hook.
10. Prosecution rises and says to the Judge that the Prosecution's case is concluded.
11. Defence makes a short opening statement to the Jury, outlining their defence and listing their witnesses: Peter Pan, Wendy Darling, and Tinker Bell.
12. Defence calls Peter Pan to the stand.
13. Prosecution cross-examines Peter.
14. Defence calls Wendy Darling to the stand.
15. Prosecution cross-examines Wendy.
16. Defence calls Tinker Bell to the stand.
17. Prosecution cross-examines Tinker Bell.
18. Defence rises and says to the Judge that the Defence case is concluded.
19. Defence makes a closing statement to the Judge and Jury.
20. Prosecution makes a closing statement to the Judge and Jury.
21. The Judge makes a brief statement to the Jury, reviewing the charges and instructs them to go to the Jury room to decide their verdict.
22. Sheriff 2 says "Order in the court. All rise."
23. The Judge and the Jury exit the courtroom.
24. The Jury deliberates.
25. Sheriff 2 says "Order in the court. All rise."
26. The Judge and Jury return to the courtroom, accompanied by Sheriff 2.
27. The Judge asks the Jury for the verdict.
28. The Foreperson reads out the verdict of guilty or not guilty for each charge. If Peter Pan is found guilty of any charge, the Judge will impose an appropriate sentence. Otherwise, the Judge tells Peter that he is free to go.
27. The Court Clerk adjourns the court.

Trial Script

Sheriff 2:	Order in the court. All rise.
	(Everyone remains standing as the Jury and then the Judge enter the courtroom.)
Court Clerk:	This court is now in session. Mr./Madam Justice _____ presiding.
Judge:	You may be seated.
	(All participants sit. Sheriff 1 is seated by Peter Pan; Sheriff 2 sits between the Judge and Jury.)
	Are all parties present?
Prosecution 1:	*(Stands and addresses the Judge)* Yes, My Lord/My Lady. In the case of Her Majesty the Queen against Peter Pan, I am _____, and with me are _____ and _____, acting on behalf of the Prosecution.
	(Each member of the Prosecution stands as he/she is introduced; all sit after introductions are finished.)
Judge:	Thank you. *(Looks at Defence.)*
Defence 1:	*(Stands and addresses the Judge)* I am _____, and with me are _____ and _____, acting on behalf of the accused, My Lord/My Lady.
	(Each member of the Defence stands as he/she is being introduced.)
Judge:	Thank you.
	(To Court Clerk) Please read the charge.
Court Clerk:	*(Stands)* Will the defendant please rise?
	(Peter Pan and Sheriff 1 stand.)
	(Reading from the indictment) Peter Pan, you stand charged that on or about April 1st, 20~~, in the City of ~~~~, in the Province/Territory of ~~~, you did unlawfully take Wendy, John, and Michael Darling to Neverland, with intent to deprive Mr. and Mrs. Darling, their parents, and Nana, the family's nurse dog, of them, contrary to section 281 of *The Criminal Code of Canada*. How do you plead?
Peter:	Not guilty, My Lord/My Lady!
Court Clerk:	My Lord/My Lady, the accused pleads not guilty to this charge.
Judge:	Thank you. You may be seated.
	(Those standing now sit down.)
	(To Prosecution) Please proceed with your case.
Prosecution 1:	*(Opening statement)* My Lord/My Lady, we intend to prove that Peter Pan deliberately entered the nursery of the Darling home that evening with the intent of taking the Darling children away with him to Neverland. He had no right to enter the nursery and if he hadn't filled the children's

heads with stories about pirates and mermaids, they would never have asked Peter to teach them to fly, and would never have agreed to go off with him to Neverland.

To support our case we will be calling the Arresting Officer; Nana, the Newfoundland dog who was the family nursemaid; and Captain Hook as witnesses. We now wish to call the Arresting Officer to the stand.

(The Arresting Officer enters the witness stand.)

Court Clerk:	*(Approaches the witness stand)* Do you swear to tell the truth, the whole truth, and nothing but the truth?
Arresting Officer:	I do.
Court Clerk:	State your name and address, please.
Arresting Officer:	I am the Arresting Officer and my regular beat is Kensington Gardens, the neighborhood around the Darlings' home.
Court Clerk:	Thank you.
	(The Court Clerk returns to his/her seat.)
Prosecution 1:	Officer, have you been a member of the police force for very long?
Arresting Officer:	Yes sir/ma'am, for many years.
Prosecution 1:	Do you know the neighborhood around the Darling home well?
Arresting Officer:	Yes. I have been patrolling that area for many years, and I know all the comings and goings of the people in my neighborhood well, especially the Darling family.
Prosecution 1:	Have you been called to deal with disturbances in that area before?
Arresting Officer:	No. It is usually a very peaceful neighborhood.
Prosecution 1:	I see. Well, Officer, please tell the court what happened on the evening in question.
Arresting Officer:	I was walking my regular beat past the Darlings' home when I heard a disturbance through the nursery window.
Prosecution 1:	What did you do?
Arresting Officer:	I knocked on the front door and the maid let me in and took me upstairs to the nursery.
Prosecution 1:	What did you find when you got there?

Arresting Officer:	The entire Darling family, Nana, their Newfoundland dog, and Peter Pan and his companion Tinker Bell were in the nursery.
Prosecution 1:	What were they doing?
Arresting Officer:	Mrs. Darling was dancing around the room, hugging all the children, Mr. Darling was welcoming them home, and Nana was holding on to Peter's shadow so he couldn't get away.
Prosecution 1:	Had you known that the Darling children were missing?
Arresting Officer:	Oh yes. Mr. and Mrs. Darling informed me on the night they flew away, and we've all been looking high and low for them ever since.
Prosecution 1:	Did you find any evidence in the nursery the night that they went missing?
Arresting Officer:	Yes. We took fingerprints from the fireplace mantle and the ceiling.
Prosecution 1:	Do those fingerprints match those of anyone in this courtroom today?
Arresting Officer:	Yes sir/ma'am. They match those of the Darling children and Peter Pan.

Prosecution 1:	(Holding up a fingerprint chart) Are these the fingerprints you took that night?
Arresting Officer:	Yes, they are.
Prosecution 1:	*(To Judge)* My Lord/My Lady, we would like to submit these finger prints as Exhibit 1.

(He/she hands the fingerprint chart to the Court Clerk.)

(The Court Clerk labels the fingerprint chart "Exhibit 1," then shows it to the Jury before showing it to the Judge.)

And Officer, did you find any evidence in the nursery the night that the children returned? |
| Arresting Officer: | Yes, I found some dust sprinkled on the heads and shoulders of Wendy, John, and Michael. They told me it was fairy dust and Peter Pan had sprinkled it on them so they could fly. |

Prosecution 1:	Is this the dust you collected that night, Officer?
	(He/she picks up a plastic bag containing a glittery powder.)
Arresting Officer:	Yes, sir/ma'am, that's it there.
Prosecution 1:	*(To Judge)* My Lord/My Lady, we would like to submit this fairy dust as Exhibit 2.
Judge:	Exhibit accepted.
	(The Court Clerk labels the plastic bag "Exhibit 2," then shows it to the Jury before showing it to the Judge.)
Prosecution 1:	Officer, did Peter Pan look like he was going to try and sneak away?
Defence 1:	*(Standing and facing the Judge)* My Lord/My Lady, we object!
	Prosecution is leading the witness!
Judge:	Objection sustained. (Judge may comment further.)
Prosecution 1:	I will rephrase my question, My Lord/My Lady. Officer, what happened next?
Arresting Officer:	Nana was still holding Peter by his shadow. Mr. and Mrs. Darling asked Peter if he'd like to come and live with them.
Prosecution 1:	And how did he reply?
Arresting Officer:	He said he wanted to go back to Neverland and he never wanted to grow up. He said he hoped Wendy would want to come back at least one week every spring.
Prosecution 1:	Is this when you took Peter Pan into custody?
Arresting Officer:	Yes.
Prosecution 1:	Thank you, Officer.
	(To Judge) No further questions, My Lord/My Lady.
Judge:	*(To Defence)* Does the Defence wish to cross-examine?
Defence 1:	Yes, My Lord/My Lady.
	Officer, did you see Peter Pan and the Darling children fly at any time?
Arresting Officer:	Well, no, I can't say I did, sir/ma'am
Defence 1:	How did Peter Pan seem to be getting along with the Darling children?
Arresting Officer:	Very well; the children seemed to like Peter very much.

Defence 1:	Did Peter come along to the station with you willingly?
Arresting Officer:	Yes, he said he was looking forward to it – he thought it would be quite an adventure.
Defence 1:	And Officer, has Peter ever been in trouble with the law before?
Arresting Officer:	Not to my knowledge.
Defence 1:	Thank you.
	(To Judge) No further questions, My Lord/My Lady.
Judge:	You may step down, Officer.
	(To Prosecution) Please call your next witness.
Prosecution 2:	We call Nana, the Darlings' nurse, to the stand, My Lord/My Lady.
	(Nana enters the witness stand.)
Court Clerk:	*(Approaches the witness stand)* Do you swear to tell the truth, the whole truth, and nothing but the truth?
Nana:	I do.
Court Clerk:	State your name and address please.
Nana:	My name is Nana and I live with the Darling family at 14 Kensington Lane.
Court Clerk:	Thank you. You may be seated.
	(Nana sits down in the witness stand. The Court Clerk returns to his/her seat.)
Prosecution 2:	Nana, what is your job with the Darling family?
Nana:	I am the family nursemaid. It is my job to escort the children to school each day. I always carry an umbrella in my mouth and make sure they walk in a proper manner.
Prosecution 2:	And what other duties do you have?
Nana:	It is my duty to make sure the children take their baths and conduct themselves properly in the nursery. I help give them their cough medicine and tuck them in at night.
Prosecution 2:	Had Wendy, John, and Michael ever disappeared before?
Nana:	No.
Prosecution 2:	And where were you that evening?

Nana:	It was my night off, and I was in my doghouse in the yard.
Prosecution 2:	Did you see anything?
Nana:	Yes. I knew Mrs. Darling was telling the children a bedtime story, and I could see Peter Pan and his little friend Tinker Bell sitting on the ledge outside the nursery window, listening.
Prosecution 2:	Did you see them go through the open window?
Nana:	Yes. After Mrs. Darling left the room, only one nightlight stayed on, and that's when I saw Peter and Tinker Bell enter the room.
Prosecution 2:	What did you do?
Nana:	I barked, but no one paid any attention to me.
Prosecution 2:	Then what did you see?
Nana:	After a little while I saw shadows on the curtains. It looked like the children were flying about the room!
Prosecution 2:	Was Peter Pan leading them?
Defence 2:	Objection, My Lord/My Lady! Calls for speculation on the part of Nana.
Judge:	Objection sustained. Ask the question differently.
Prosecution 2:	*(To Judge)* Sorry, My Lord/My Lady. (To Nana) How long did this go on?
Nana:	They seemed to be practising flying up to the ceiling for a short while, then all of a sudden I heard a shout and they all came flying out the window.
Prosecution 2:	Who did you hear shouting?
Nana:	It was Peter Pan.
Prosecution 2:	What did he say?
Nana:	He shouted, "Off we go to Neverland! Second to the right and straight on till morning!"
Prosecution 2:	Did you notice who was leading the way?
Nana:	Peter Pan was first, followed by Wendy, then John in his best Sunday hat, and finally little Michael.
Prosecution 2:	What did you do?
Nana:	I went dashing into the house to get Mr. and Mrs. Darling, but by then it was too late. They were gone!
Prosecution 2:	Did you help look for the children?

Nana:	Yes, we looked everywhere, but there was no trace of where they had gone. None of us knew the way to Neverland, and besides, we couldn't fly.
Prosecution 2:	Were the children gone for a long time?
Nana:	It seemed like forever.
Prosecution 2:	What happened on the evening they returned?
Nana:	Mrs. Darling had fallen asleep in the rocking chair in the nursery, and I was lying at her feet when all of a sudden the children came flying back through the window.
Prosecution 2:	It was a good thing the window was open!
Nana:	It was always left open so the children could return.
Prosecution 2:	What happened when they came in?
Nana:	I jumped up barking. I was so happy to see them. Mrs. Darling woke up and started dancing around the room, and Mr. Darling came racing in to see what all the commotion was about.
Prosecution 2:	Were the children happy to be home?
Nana:	They were very excited and wanted to tell their parents all about their adventures in Neverland. I saw Peter about to slip out the window, so I grabbed his shadow.
Prosecution 2:	*(Holding Peter's shadow towards Nana)* Is this the same shadow?
Nana:	*(Looking it over)* Yes, it has my bite marks on it.
Prosecution 2:	My Lord/My Lady, we would like to submit this shadow as Exhibit 3. *(He/she hands the shadow to the Court Clerk. The Court Clerk labels the shadow "Exhibit 3," then shows it to the Jury before showing it to the Judge.)*
Judge:	Thank you. Exhibit accepted.
Prosecution 2:	What did you do then, Nana?
Nana:	I held on to Peter's shadow until the Arresting Officer arrived.
Prosecution 2:	Thank you, Nana. No further questions, My Lord/My Lady.
Judge:	(To Defence) Does the Defence wish to cross-examine?

Defence 2:	Yes, My Lord/My Lady.
	Nana, had you ever seen Peter Pan in the nursery before?
Nana:	No, but the children had often mentioned him from their dreams and I sometimes wondered if someone was outside the nursery window while Mrs. Darling told them their bedtime stories.
Defence 2:	But you can't say for sure if it was Peter Pan?
Nana:	Well … no.
Defence 2:	And how did the children seem when they returned?
Nana:	Very happy and excited!
Defence 2:	Don't you think it was very kind of Peter to bring the children back from Neverland?
Nana:	Yes, I suppose it was.
Defence 2:	And obviously Peter had taken good care of the children while they were in Neverland, if they returned in such good spirits?
Prosecution 2:	*(To Judge)* My Lord/My Lady, we object!
Judge:	On what grounds?
Prosecution 2:	That calls for conjecture on the part of the witness. Nana can't say this for sure.
Judge	Objection sustained.
Defence 2:	Nana, it doesn't seem very kind of you to bite off Peter's shadow after he'd brought the children back.
Nana:	I was only trying to hold him to keep from flying away. I thought Mr. and Mrs. Darling would want to speak to him.
Defence 2:	Did Peter try to get away?
Nana:	No. He seemed to be enjoying all the excitement!
Defence 2:	Thank you. No further questions, My Lord/My Lady.
Judge:	*(To Nana)* Thank you. You may step down.
	(To Prosecution) You may call your next witness.
Prosecution 3:	Thank you My Lord/My Lady. We now call Captain Hook to the stand.
	(Captain Hook enters the witness stand.)
Court Clerk:	*(Approaches the witness stand)* Do you swear to tell the truth, the whole truth, and nothing but the truth?
Capt. Hook:	I do.
Court Clerk:	State your name and address, please.

Capt. Hook:	My name is Captain James Hook and I live on my ship, the Jolly Roger, in Neverland.
Court Clerk:	Thank you. You may be seated.
	(Captain Hook sits down in the witness stand. The Court Clerk returns to his/her seat.)
Prosecution 3:	Captain Hook, do you know the boy Peter Pan well?
Hook:	Unfortunately, yes.
Prosecution 3:	Why do you say "unfortunately"?
Capt. Hook:	Because that boy has been a bother to me for quite a while! He is always getting up to some sort of mischief in Neverland.
Prosecution 3:	Do you see that boy in the courtroom today?
Capt. Hook:	Yes! (He points with his hook to Peter Pan.)
Prosecution 3:	*(To the Judge)* May the record show that the witness has identified the accused.
	Has Peter brought other children to Neverland?
Capt. Hook:	Yes – lots of times.
Prosecution 3:	Do you see any of those children in the courtroom today?
Capt. Hook:	Yes. They came to visit my ship towards the end of their stay in Neverland. *(He points to Wendy, John, and Michael.)*
Prosecution 3:	*(To Judge)* Let the record show that Captain Hook has identified Wendy, John, and Michael Darling.
	And did Peter come with them to visit your ship?
Capt. Hook:	No, he was sleeping.
Prosecution 3:	Do you recall what the Darling children talked about when you were with them?
Capt. Hook:	They seemed to talk a lot about their parents. I had the impression that they missed their mother, especially, but Peter wouldn't let them go home.
Prosecution 3:	Thank you. No further questions, My Lord/My Lady.
Judge:	Does the Defence wish to cross-examine?
Defence 3:	Yes, My Lord/My Lady.

	Captain Hook, I suggest that it is you who is always trying to cause mischief on Neverland and not Peter Pan! Isn't it true that you and your pirates are always creeping onto the island and trying to catch Peter and the other children unawares?
Prosecution 3:	My Lord/My Lady, I object!
Judge:	Objection overruled. Please answer the question, Captain Hook.
Capt. Hook:	It's only in fun. It's a game. We don't mean any harm.
Defence 3:	And isn't it true that the evening you took Wendy, John, and Michael back to the Jolly Roger you tied them to the mast and said you were going to make them walk the gang-plank if Peter didn't rescue them?
Capt. Hook:	It was only a joke.
Defence 3:	And isn't it true that you put something in Peter's medicine that night so that when he took it he would not be able to rescue the children?
Capt. Hook:	Well, I don't know if he took the medicine. Besides . . . he did rescue them!
Defence 3:	So you admit that you did take the Darlings prisoners! And Peter was able to rescue them only because he did not take the medicine. Members of the Jury, it is obvious that Captain Hook's testimony is not trustworthy and it is in his interests to keep Peter out of Neverland.
Prosecution 3:	My Lord/My Lady I object. It is up to the Jury to decide if Captain Hook is trustworthy.
Judge:	Objection sustained.
Defence 3:	No further questions, My Lord/My Lady.
Judge:	*(To Captain Hook)* You may step down.
	(Captain Hook returns to his seat in the courtroom.)
	(To Prosecution) Do you wish to call any further witnesses?
Prosecution 3:	No, My Lord/My Lady. We rest our case.
Judge:	*(To Defence)* You may give your opening statement.
Defence 1	Thank you, My Lord/My Lady.

(Opening statement) We intend to show that Peter did not intentionally enter the Darling nursery to entice the children to fly away with him to Neverland. He had been listening at the window because he enjoyed Mrs. Darling's bedtime stories and that night he slipped into the room to search for his missing shadow. The Darling children woke up accidentally – Peter didn't intend to wake them – and asked that he teach them to fly. Wendy offered to go to Neverland so she could tell Peter and the lost boys stories, and tuck them into their beds at night.

To support our case, we will be calling Peter Pan, Wendy Darling, and Tinker Bell to the stand as witnesses. We now call Peter Pan.

(Peter Pan enters the witness stand. Sheriff 1 accompanies Peter to the stand and stands beside him.)

Court Clerk:	*(Approaches the witness stand)* Do you swear to tell the truth, the whole truth, and nothing but the truth?
Peter:	I do.
Court Clerk:	State your name and address, please.
Peter:	My name is Peter Pan, and I live in Neverland.
Court Clerk:	Thank you. You may be seated.

(Peter Pan sits down in the witness stand. The Court Clerk returns to his/her seat.)

Defence 1:	Peter, were you in the habit of visiting the Darling home often?
Peter:	Sometimes Tinker Bell and I would visit before bedtime, so we could sit on the windowsill and listen to Mrs. Darling's stories.
Defence 1:	Had you ever entered the nursery before?
Peter:	No.
Defence 1:	Why did you enter the nursery on the night in question?
Peter:	I had lost my shadow and Tinker Bell and I were looking for it.
Defence:	Did you find your shadow?
Peter:	Yes, but I couldn't get it back on again. I tried sticking it on with soap, but that didn't work.
Defence 1:	So how did you finally attach it?
Peter:	Wendy woke up while I was trying to stick it on and she very kindly sewed it back on for me.

Defence 1:	Now, Peter, whose idea was it to teach Wendy, John, and Michael to fly?
Peter:	It was Wendy's idea. She thought it would be so lovely if they could fly about the room.
Defence 1:	How did you teach them?
Peter:	I just told them to think happy thoughts, and then I sprinkled some of Tinker Bell's fairy dust on them.
Defence 1:	And Peter, whose idea was it that the children go with you to Neverland?
Peter:	Wendy's. She said she could come and tell us lovely bedtime stories and tuck us in at night, me and the lost boys.
Defence 1:	Did you deliberately try to trick the Darling children into flying off to Neverland with you?
Peter:	No. They wanted to come and have adventures with the pirates and mermaids. And I couldn't make them fly if they didn't want to – all I did was teach them how.
Defence 1:	Did it not occur to you, Peter, that their parents and Nana would miss them very much?
Peter:	They were only coming for a visit.
Defence 1:	And did you and the children have lots of adventures in Neverland?
Peter:	Yes! We went swimming with the mermaids, searched for buried treasure at the lagoon, and Wendy told us lots of lovely bedtime stories and tucked us all in at night.
Defence 1:	When did you decide that it was time to return?
Peter:	It was after that awful Captain Hook tricked Wendy, John, and Michael and threatened to have them walk the plank on the Jolly Roger.
Defence 1:	How did you save them, Peter?
Peter:	I climbed aboard the ship and made a ticking sound. Captain Hook thought I was the crocodile that had eaten his hand, and was very frightened! While he was hiding, I rescued Wendy, John, and Michael.
Defence 1:	They must have been very thankful.
Peter:	Yes, but they said they were tired of having adventures, so I agreed to show them the way back from Neverland.
Defence 1:	And what happened when you arrived back?
Peter:	The children flew into the nursery and Nana started to bark. Mrs. Darling was asleep in the rocking chair, and Mr.

Darling came running in to see what all the commotion was about.

Defence 1:	Did you try to get away?
Peter:	I didn't feel I belonged. I was rather sad that Wendy and John and Michael would no longer be in Neverland but I knew they were happy to be back.
Defence 1:	So what did you do?
Peter:	I tried to slip out the window with Tinker Bell, but Nana saw me and grabbed on to my shadow! I didn't want to lose it again, so I didn't try to pull away.
Defence 1:	Were the Darling parents angry with you?
Peter:	I don't think so. They were glad to have the children back and Wendy introduced me. They asked if I would like to stay.
Defence 1:	What did you say?
Peter:	I told them I wanted to go back to Neverland and that I didn't ever want to grow up.
Defence 1:	Thank you, Peter. No further questions, My Lord/My Lady.
Judge:	Does the Prosecution wish to cross-examine?
Prosecution 1:	Yes, My Lord/My Lady.
	Peter, isn't it true that you asked Wendy to come to Neverland so she could tell lots of bedtime stories?
Peter:	Only after she offered.
Prosecution 1:	And isn't it also true that you made the children want to learn how to fly by showing off and flying all around the nursery with Tinker Bell?
Peter:	They asked. It was Michael's idea to try to fly out the window.
Prosecution 1:	And whose idea was it to fly all the way to Neverland?
Peter:	It was Wendy's idea.
Prosecution 1:	And didn't you care that their parents would be upset and miss them?
Peter:	But the children wanted to have lots of wonderful adventures, and we weren't going to be gone for long.
Prosecution 1:	On the night you returned, isn't it a fact that you tried to slip away because you knew Mr. and Mrs. Darling would be angry with you?
Peter:	No!
Prosecution 1:	If it hadn't been for Nana grabbing your shadow, you'd have been gone! Peter, did you even think to apologize to Mr. and Mrs. Darling?

Peter:	I think Mrs. Darling knows that all children visit Neverland in their dreams. There didn't seem to be any need – everyone was just so happy to be together again.
Prosecution 1:	Well, thank you, Peter Pan. No further questions, My Lord/My Lady.
Judge:	*(To Peter Pan)* You may step down.
	(Peter Pan returns to his seat. Sheriff 1 accompanies him.)
	(To Defence) You may call your next witness.
Defence 2:	Thank you, My Lord/My Lady. We now call Wendy to the stand.
	(Wendy enters the witness stand.)
Court Clerk:	*(Approaches the witness stand)* Do you swear to tell the truth, the whole truth, and nothing but the truth?
Wendy:	I do.
Court Clerk:	State your name and address, please.
Wendy:	My name is Wendy Moira Angela Darling and I am ~~ years old. I live with my parents, Nana, and my brothers John and Michael at number 14, Kensington Lane.
Court Clerk:	Thank you. You may be seated.
	(Wendy sits in the witness stand. The Court Clerk returns to his/her seat.)
Defence 2:	Wendy, when was the first time you were aware of the boy called Peter Pan?
Wendy:	Sometimes when I woke up I'd almost remember a boy named Peter from my dreams.
Defence 2:	Did you ever talk about him with anyone?
Wendy:	Yes, sometimes John, who is eight, and Michael, who is six, and I would tell each other about our dreams of Neverland and we'd compare our stories.
Defence 2:	Did you all have the same dreams?
Wendy:	No. I'd dream of mermaids, John would dream of pirate ships, and Michael would dream about a lagoon full of flamingos. But Peter was in all our dreams.
Defence 2:	Wendy, did you know that Peter Pan sometimes came from Neverland to sit on the window ledge of your nursery so that he and Tinker Bell could listen to your mother's bedtime stories?
Wendy:	I didn't know that until the night he came into the nursery.
Defence 2:	Were you frightened when you woke up and found Peter flying about your room?
Wendy:	No, I felt as if I knew him already.

Defence 2:	What did Peter say to you?
Wendy:	He said he was looking for his shadow. He had a lovely little fairy helping him, and she was like a little light flying about the room.
Defence 2:	Did you help him find his shadow?
Wendy:	Tinker Bell found it, but I helped sew it on.
Defence 2:	What happened next, Wendy?
Wendy:	John and Michael woke up and we were all very excited! Peter and Tinker Bell were flying about the room.
Defence 2:	Wendy, whose idea was it to teach you and John and Michael to fly?
Wendy:	I believe I asked Peter if we might be able to try flying about the room.
Defence 2:	And whose idea was it to try flying out the window?
Wendy:	Michael's. He wanted to fly about the church spire.
Defence 2:	Now Wendy, this is a very important question, so please think carefully before you answer. Whose suggestion was it that you all fly off to Neverland?
Wendy:	I think I was the one who said it would be delightful if we could all go off with Peter.
Defence 2:	Why?
Wendy:	So we could have adventures also. I wanted to see the mermaids I'd seen in my dreams.
Defence 2:	What about John and Michael?
Wendy:	They wanted to see the pirate ship and flamingos.
Defence 2:	Wendy, did Peter try to persuade you children to go with him?
Wendy:	He didn't have to – we all wanted to go to Neverland.
Defence 2:	And was it difficult to get Peter to bring you back home?
Wendy:	For a while we were having such fun that no one thought about coming back.
Defence 2:	What changed your mind?
Wendy:	When that horrible Captain Hook captured us and took us to the Jolly Roger! He threatened to tie us all to a mast! I was very worried about John and Michael.
Defence 2:	Wendy, were your mother and father happy when you returned?
Wendy:	Yes, very! Mother especially seemed to understand that we had had a lovely adventure. She even asked Peter if he would like to stay with us.
Defence 2:	But Peter has decided he'd rather live in Neverland.

Wendy:	Yes, but I'm hoping that Mother will let me go back for a week every spring to visit.
Defence 2:	Thank you, Wendy. No further questions, My Lord/My Lady.
Judge:	Does the Prosecution wish to cross-examine?
Prosecution 2:	Yes, My Lord/My Lady.
	Wendy, would you ever have thought about flying off to Neverland if Peter had not come in to the nursery that evening?
Wendy:	Well, probably not, but it was a lovely thing to do.
Prosecution 2:	And weren't you worried about John and Michael being away from home?
Wendy:	Well, being the eldest, I was looking after them, but I did start to worry after a while.
Prosecution 2:	Why was that?
Wendy:	Because they seemed to be forgetting about our home.
Prosecution 2:	Whose suggestion was it that you all return from Neverland? Was it yours or Peter's?
Wendy:	I don't remember. Maybe we all thought of it at the same time.
Prosecution 2:	No further questions, My Lord/My Lady.
Judge:	You may step down, Wendy.
	(Wendy returns to her seat in the courtroom.)
	(To Defence) Do you wish to call any other witnesses?
Defence 3:	Yes, My Lord/My Lady. We wish to call Tinker Bell to the stand.
	(Tinker Bell enters the witness stand.)
Court Clerk:	*(Approaches the witness stand)* Do you swear to tell the truth, the whole truth, and nothing but the truth?
Tinker Bell:	I do.
Court Clerk:	State your name and address, please.
Tinker Bell:	My name is Tinker Bell, and I live in Neverland.
Court Clerk:	Thank you. You may be seated.
	(Tinker Bell sits down in the witness stand. The Court Clerk returns to his/her seat.)
Defence 3:	Tinker Bell, have you known Peter Pan for long?

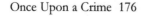

Tinker Bell:	Yes, years and years. He is a good friend.
Defence 3:	Did you often go with Peter to listen at nursery windows?
Tinker Bell:	Quite often. We don't have anyone to tell us bedtime stories in Neverland.
Defence 3:	What happened on the night in question?
Tinker Bell:	We were listening through the Darlings' window when Peter noticed that his shadow was missing.
Defence 3:	What did you do?
Tinker Bell:	We waited until only the nightlights were on and the children were sleeping, and then we slipped into the room.
Defence 3:	Did Peter deliberately wake up the children?
Tinker Bell:	No! We were searching everywhere and Peter accidentally shut me into a closet. I'm afraid I must have been too noisy and woke them up.
Defence 3:	As far as you can remember, Tinker Bell, whose idea was it to teach Wendy, John, and Michael to fly?
Tinker Bell:	Wendy's!
Defence 3:	And did Peter try to persuade the children to fly off to Neverland with both of you?
Tinker Bell:	No. It was the children's idea.
Defence 3:	Tinker Bell, has Peter always been a good friend?
Tinker Bell:	Yes – in fact, he even saved my life.
Defence 3:	Can you tell us about that?
Tinker Bell:	Well, that horrible Captain Hook had come to capture the children when Peter was sleeping. Captain Hook put something into Peter's medicine so that Peter couldn't fly off to the Jolly Roger to rescue them. When he woke up, he was going to drink his medicine, so I drank it instead to save him.
Defence 3:	That was very courageous of you.
Tinker Bell:	Thank you – I just couldn't let Peter take it.
Defence 3:	What happened next?
Tinker Bell:	Well, I became very sick and almost died. But Peter called on all the sleeping children who were dreaming of Neverland to clap their hands if they believed in fairies. And it worked! When all those children clapped their hands, I got better. It was because of them, and Peter, that I'm still here. I'll always be grateful to Peter for that.
Defence 3:	Thank you. No further questions, My Lord/My Lady.
Judge:	Does the Prosecution wish to cross-examine the witness?

Prosecution 3:	Yes, My Lord/My Lady.
	Tinker Bell, how does one learn to fly?
Tinker Bell:	You just think happy thoughts.
Prosecution 3:	Isn't there something else?
Tinker Bell:	Oh, yes … you also need some fairy dust.
Prosecution 3:	So, if you hadn't lent Peter some fairy dust for Wendy, John, and Michael, they wouldn't have been able to fly away to Neverland?
Tinker Bell:	Well, I guess not.
Prosecution 3:	In fact, if you hadn't made so much noise that night, looking for Peter's shadow, the children might never have awakened and met Peter?
Tinker Bell:	I suppose not, but I was only trying to help.
Prosecution 3:	Do you always do everything that Peter tells you to?
Tinker Bell:	Of course not. But he can be lots of fun at times.
Prosecution 3:	And do you think Peter deliberately encouraged Wendy, John, and Michael to fly off to Neverland with the two of you?
Tinker Bell:	No! He was only inviting them for a visit so they could have an adventure.
Prosecution 3:	I see. That is all. No further questions, My Lord/My Lady.
Judge:	You may step down, Tinker Bell.
	(Tinker Bell returns to her seat in the courtroom.)
	(To Defence) Do you wish to call any further witnesses?
Defence 3:	No, My Lord/My Lady. We rest our case.
Judge:	Thank you. You may begin your summations.
Defence 3:	Thank you, My Lord/My Lady.

(Closing statement) Ladies and gentlemen of the Jury, it is the duty of the Prosecution to prove to you, beyond a reasonable doubt that Peter not only encouraged Wendy, John, and Michael to fly off with him to Neverland, but that he intended to do so.

In fact, Peter did not come to the Darlings' home to cause trouble. The nursery window was always left open, and Peter came to listen through the window to Mrs. Darling's bedtime stories. The night he entered, he was looking for his shadow. When Peter told Wendy about Neverland, she offered to come to tell bedtime stories. All three children wanted to learn to fly and asked Peter to take them to Neverland so they could have adventures. It is the argument of the Defence that the children flew off willingly and that Peter did not deliberately encourage them to leave home. It was always Peter's intention to return the children to their nursery after they had enjoyed their adventures. We also contend that Wendy, John, and Michael must carry some responsibility for these proceedings. We have shown that it was the children's idea to fly off to Neverland. We feel that Peter has already been sufficiently punished for any errors in judgment, and ask that you find him not guilty and allow him to return to Neverland with Tinker Bell. Thank you.

Judge:	*(To Defence)* Thank you.
	(To Prosecution) Would the Prosecution please deliver its closing statement to the Jury.
Prosecution 3:	Thank you, My Lord/My Lady.

(Closing statement) Ladies and gentlemen of the Jury, we believe that we have shown beyond a reasonable doubt that Peter should be found guilty under section 281 of *The Criminal Code of Canada* entitled "Abduction of person under 14."

We feel the Prosecution has shown that Peter did encourage Wendy, John, and Michael to fly away with him to Neverland, thus depriving their parents and nursemaid from having them at home where they rightfully belonged. The Prosecution will also remind the court that section 286 of *The Criminal Code of Canada* states that it is not a defence to any charge that a young person consented to, or suggested, any conduct of the accused. Therefore, Peter cannot use as a defence the suggestion that the children asked to be taught to fly, and to go with Peter to Neverland.

We also remind you that at no time has Peter shown any remorse for the pain and grief he caused Mr. and Mrs. Darling and Nana. We ask that you set an example to all children who might consider flying off to Neverland, and find Peter guilty. Thank you.

Judge: *(To Prosecution)* Thank you.

(To Jury) As members of the Jury, you will have to make a decision of whether Peter is guilty or not guilty for the charge that he did unlawfully take Wendy, John, and Michael Darling to Neverland, with intent to deprive Mr. and Mrs. Darling, their parents, and Nana, the family's nurse dog, of them, contrary to section 281 of *The Criminal Code of Canada*.

Think about what the witnesses and lawyers said during the trial. Your job is to carefully weigh the evidence from both the prosecution and defence witnesses and lawyers and come to a decision. You need to decide which witnesses are more believable and which argument is most plausible. You will then vote on each charge. For this trial, your Jury is only required to reach a majority decision.

You now have 15 minutes to discuss the case. When you return, I will ask your Foreperson your verdict.

Sheriff 2:	Order in the court. All rise.
	(Everyone stands.)
Court Clerk:	Court will now adjourn for 15 minutes.
	(The Judge and Jury leave the courtroom, followed by Sheriff 2.)
	(When the Judge and Jury are ready to return, approximately 15 minutes later, Sheriff 2 enters the courtroom and calls the court to order.)
Sheriff 2:	Order in the court. All rise.
	(Everyone stands as the Jury and then the Judge enter the courtroom and are seated.)
Court Clerk:	Court is now resumed. Please be seated.
	(All participants sit.)
Judge:	Mr./Madam Foreperson, have you reached a verdict?
Foreperson:	*(Stands)* Yes, My Lord/My Lady.
Court Clerk:	*(Stands)* Will the defendant please rise?
	(Peter Pan and Sheriff 1 stand.)
Judge:	*(To Foreperson)* You may read the verdict.
Foreperson:	We find the accused, Peter Pan, guilty/not guilty of the charge of unlawfully taking Wendy, John, and Michael Darling to Neverland.
Judge:	Thank you.
	(The Judge then passes sentence if Peter is found guilty of the charges, or acquits Peter if he is found not guilty of the charge.)
Sheriff 1:	*(Standing)* Order in the court. All rise.
	(All participants stand.)
Court Clerk:	This court is now adjourned.

Hansel and Gretel Mock Trial

Her Majesty the Queen v. Hansel and Gretel

By Julie Fortin

Recommended for Grades 5 to 7

Case for the Prosecution

That Hansel and Gretel caused damage to private property, namely a cottage made of sweets owned by the old witch Rosina Daintymouth, by eating pieces off the cottage. Furthermore, as Hansel and Gretel committed the crime of breaking and entering the witch's cottage. Lastly, that Hansel and Gretel committed the murder of the old witch Rosina Daintymouth and committed theft of her personal valuables.

Case for the Defence

That Hansel and Gretel have been wrongfully charged on all counts. They were lost, hungry, and tired, and they believed the cottage built of candy was uninhabited. They did not commit a break and enter for they were invited into the home. They did not commit murder: it will be shown that the witch Rosina Daintymouth was killed in self-defence. They also did not commit theft: Hansel and Gretel considered that the pearls and precious stones that they took with them were compensation for the injuries and suffering that the old witch inflicted on them.

Trial Roles

Judge (best played by an adult)

Prosecution Lawyers 1, 2, and 3
Defence Lawyers 1, 2, and 3

Prosecution Witnesses:
Ent (Talking Tree)
Wood Goblin
Grizelda Daintymouth (sister of the deceased witch Rosina Daintymouth)

Defence Witnesses:
Little Red Riding Hood
Hansel
Gretel

Officers of the Court:
Court Clerk
Court Reporter
Sheriffs 1 and 2

Members of the Jury, one of whom is appointed Foreperson)

Members of the Media:
Print journalists
Television reporters
Court artist

Suggestions for Costumes, Props, and Exhibits

Costumes

Judge	Gown
Prosecution Lawyers	Black gowns
Defence Lawyers	Black gowns
Court Clerk	Black gown
Court Reporter	Black gown
Sheriffs 1 and 2	Brown hats and jackets
Ent	Tree costume; leaves and twigs as headwear
Wood Goblin	Goblin costume
Grizelda Daintymouth	Witch costume: black pointed hat, black robe
Little Red Riding Hood	Red cape; could carry wicker basket
Hansel	Shabby farm clothes
Gretel	Shabby farm clothes
Court Artist	Smock and beret; could carry paper and coloring pencils
Members of the Media	Name tags or press identification attached to hats or jackets, or worn around the neck; could carry pens and notebooks
Members of the Jury	Farm clothing or forest animal costumes (with ears, tails, and face paint)

Props

Indictment (a sheet of paper on which the charge is written)

Exhibits

Exhibit 1:	Bag of shiny rocks
Exhibit 2:	Hair strands
Exhibit 3:	Crime scene reports
Exhibit 4:	Inventory of jewels owned by Rosina Daintymouth

Procedure

Entering the Courtroom

1. The teacher welcomes the guests and reviews the intent and format of the trial, and the role of the audience.
2. Prosecution and Defence lawyers arrive and sit at their tables.
3. The witnesses and media arrive and sit in the area reserved for them.
4. Sheriff 1 enters the courtroom with Hansel and Gretel. He/she seats Hansel and Gretel in the prisoner's box and sits nearby.
5. The Court Clerk and Court Reporter arrive and take their places.

6. Sheriff 2 calls the court to order, and asks everyone to stand.

7. The Judge and members of the Jury enter the courtroom, accompanied by Sheriff 2 and take their places. After the Judge and Jury are seated down, the public sits down and the trial is ready to begin.

Trial Procedure

1. The Court Clerk stands and reads the indictment.

2. Prosecution and Defence lawyers introduce themselves to the Judge.

3. Prosecution makes an opening statement to the Jury, presenting what they intend to prove and listing witnesses: Ent, the Wood Goblin, and Grizelda Daintymouth.

4. Prosecution calls Ent to the stand.

5. Defence cross-examines Ent.

6. Prosecution calls the Wood Goblin to the stand.

7. Defence cross-examines the Wood Goblin.

8. Prosecution calls Grizelda Daintymouth to the stand.

9. Defence cross-examines Grizelda Daintymouth.

10. Prosecution rises and says to the Judge that the Prosecution's case is concluded.

11. Defence makes an opening statement to the Jury, outlining their defence and listing their witnesses: Little Red Riding Hood, Hansel, and Gretel.

12. Defence calls Little Red Riding Hood to the stand.

13. Prosecution cross-examines Little Red Riding Hood.

14. Defence calls Hansel to the stand.

15. Prosecution cross-examines Hansel.

16. Defence calls Gretel to the stand.

17. Prosecution cross-examines Gretel.

18. Defence says to the Judge that the Defence case is concluded.

19. Defence makes a closing statement to the Judge and Jury.

20. Prosecution makes a closing statement to the Judge and Jury.

21. The Judge makes a brief statement to the Jury, reviewing the charges and instructs them to go to the Jury room to decide their verdict.

22. Sheriff 2 says "Order in the court. All rise."

23. The Judge and the Jury exit the courtroom.

24. The Jury discusses the trial.

25. Sheriff 2 says "Order in the court. All rise."

26. The Judge and Jury return, accompanied by Sheriff 2.

27. The Judge asks the Jury for the verdict

28. The Foreperson reads out the verdict of guilty or not guilty for each charge. If Hansel and Gretel are found guilty of any charge, the Judge will impose an appropriate sentence. Otherwise, the Judge tells Hansel and Gretel they are free to go.

29. The Court Clerk adjourns the court.

Trial Script

Sheriff 2:	Order in the court. All rise.
	(Everyone stands as the Jury and then the Judge enter the courtroom.)
Court Clerk:	This court is now in session. Mr./Madam Justice _____ presiding.
Judge:	You may be seated.
	(All participants sit. Sheriff 1 sits by Hansel and Gretel Sheriff 2 sits between the Judge and Jury.)
	Are all parties present?
Prosecution 1:	*(Stands and addresses the Judge)* Yes, My Lord/My Lady. In the case of Her Majesty the Queen against Hansel and Gretel, I am _____, and with me are _____ and _____, acting on behalf of the Prosecution.
	(Each member of the Prosecution stands as he/she is introduced; all sit after introductions are finished.)
Defence 1:	*(Stands and addresses the Judge)* My Lord/My Lady, I am _____, and with me are _____ and _____, acting on behalf of the accused, Hansel and Gretel.
Judge:	Thank you.
	(To Court Clerk) Please read the charges.
Court Clerk:	*(Stands)* Will the defendants please rise?
	(Hansel and Gretel, and Sheriff 1 stand.)
	(Reading from the indictment) Hansel and Gretel, you stand charged that on or about June 21st, 20~~, in Storybook Forest, in the Province/Territory of ~~~, you did commit mischief by willfully damaging property belonging to the witch Rosina Daintymouth, contrary to section 430(1) of *The Criminal Code of Canada*. How do you plead?
Hansel & Gretel:	Not guilty, My Lord/My Lady.
Court Clerk:	Hansel and Gretel, you stand charged that on or about June 21st, 20~~, in Storybook Forest, in the Province/Territory of ~~~, you did commit break and enter of the witch Rosina Daintymouth's residence, with intent to commit an indictable offence therein, contrary to section 348(1)(a) of *The Criminal Code of Canada*. How do you plead?
Hansel & Gretel:	Not guilty, My Lord/My Lady.

Court Clerk:	Hansel and Gretel, you stand charged that on or about July 14th, 20~~, in Storybook Forest, in the Province/Territory of ~~~, you did commit the murder of the witch Rosina Daintymouth, contrary to section 229 of *The Criminal Code of Canada*. How do you plead?
Hansel & Gretel:	Not guilty, My Lord/My Lady.
Court Clerk:	Hansel and Gretel, you stand charged that on or about July 14th, 20~~, in Storybook Forest, in the Province/Territory of ~~~, you did commit theft over $5 000 of pearls and precious stones belonging to the witch Rosina Daintymouth, contrary to section 334(a) of *The Criminal Code of Canada*. How do you plead?
Hansel & Gretel:	Not guilty, My Lord/My Lady.
Court Clerk:	My Lord/My Lady, the accused plead not guilty to all charges.
Judge:	Thank you. You may be seated.
	(Those standing now sit down.)
	Prosecution, please proceed with your case.
Prosecution 1:	*(Opening statement)* My Lord/My Lady, we intend to prove that Hansel and Gretel knowingly set out to maliciously damage and vandalize the private property of the old Witch. The dubious premise that the children were left alone in the forest is highly unlikely, and we intend to prove that there was a premeditated action of breaking and entering, followed by the murder of the old witch Rosina Daintymouth for personal gain from the theft of her jewels. To support our case, we will be calling Ent, the Wood Goblin, and Grizelda Daintymouth, the deceased victim's sister, as witnesses.
	We now wish to call Ent to the stand.
	(Ent enters the witness stand.)
Court Clerk:	*(Approaches the witness stand)*. Do you swear to tell the truth, the whole truth, and nothing but the truth?
Ent:	I do.
Court Clerk:	State your name and address, please.
Ent:	People call me Ent, and I live in Storybook Forest.
Court Clerk:	Thank you.
	(The Court Clerk returns to his/her seat.)
Prosecution 1:	Mr./Madam Ent, could you please explain to the courtroom what it is you are exactly?

Ent:	Of course. I am a walking willow tree. When I feel like resting or drinking, I am stationary, or rooted to the ground. When I want to move around, catch some sunshine, or visit my family, I lift up my roots and walk.
Prosecution 1:	Do you do this often?
Ent:	Oh, absolutely! It is what I do. My roots will fall off if I remain stationary and besides, I get bored easily.
Prosecution 1:	Mr./Madam Ent, have you ever witnessed people damaging the forest?
Ent:	Oh, yes. I witness it every day. Humans leave garbage, light fires without being careful, and pollute forest rivers and streams – and all of these cause plants and animals to die.
Prosecution 1:	Have you ever seen the defendants, Hansel and Gretel, in Storybook Forest?
Ent:	As a matter of fact, yes. I've seen them twice. Once, when I was on my way to visit my mother in the Forest of Avalon, they were building a fire that seemed too large to be contained by two little children, but they didn't seem to care. It could have caused a catastrophe! And another time, when I was resting near the Daintymouth witches' home, Hansel and Gretel ran up to the cottage and began breaking off pieces from the roof and window of the cottage to eat!
Prosecution 1:	And this disturbed you?
Ent:	Well, I've never really met either of the witches, but I know that I would not want my cottage destroyed by a couple of hooligans! I mean, if children came up to me and began ripping my bark off, it would both hurt me and cause damage to my complexion, just as it obviously hurt and damaged the witches' cottage.
Defence 1:	Objection – speculation.
Judge:	Objection sustained. The jury should disregard that last remark.
	(To Ent) Please confine your testimony to what you actually saw.
Prosecution 1:	Now, about this fire – do you know if it got out of hand and spread out of control?
Ent:	Word around the forest is that it did not get out of control, but my point is that it could have, and furthermore, could have killed my family and me!
Defence 1:	Objection, My Lord/My Lady! Hearsay!
Judge:	Let the Jury disregard the previous statement from the witness.
Prosecution 1:	Ent, while you were resting outside the witches' home, did you hear her invite the children inside?

Ent:	Invite those ungrateful children in the cottage? No, never! She opened the door to see what the hullabaloo was all about, and the minute that those children noticed that the door was open, they barged right in!
Prosecution 1:	Thank you, My Lord/My Lady, no further questions.
Judge:	Does Defence wish to cross examine?
Defence 1:	Yes, My Lord/My Lady, we do.
	Ent, are you familiar with the term "accessory to arson"?
Ent:	Why, whatever do you mean?
Defence 1:	Come now, Mr./Madam Ent. I am sure you are aware of the rules of the forest. Neglecting to report a large fire to the Forest Elves is a federal offence punishable by banishment!
Ent:	What are you getting at?
Defence 1:	Records show that you never reported this "uncontainable fire" that you supposedly witnessed. Are you quite sure that it was too large to be contained by two small children?
Prosecution 1:	Objection, My Lord/My Lady – the Defence is badgering the witness!
Defence 1:	My Lord/My Lady, I am merely attempting to shed light on just how credible this witness is!
Judge:	Objection overruled. Answer the question, Mr./Madam Ent.
Defence 1:	Thank you, My Lord/My Lady.
Ent:	Of course I am sure that the fire was too big to be contained – I know what's safe for my own forest!
Defence 1:	Yet, you didn't report this possible "catastrophe" … interesting. Now you mentioned earlier that Hansel and Gretel were vandalizing the witches' house and that you witnessed them running toward the cottage and consuming pieces of candy that they broke off the cottage. Did you speak to the children?
Ent:	No, I was too busy resting my roots and grooming my leaves.
Defence 1:	So you did not know whether they had permission or not to do this?
Ent:	Well, I suppose not. I only speculated that they didn't because I didn't see the Witch.
Defence 1:	Did you try to stop the children from this vandalism?
Ent:	No, I did not.

Defence 1:	Ent, are you familiar with the term "accessory to vandalism"? Actually, Mr./Madam Ent … you need not answer that.
	The Defence rests, My Lord/My Lady. No further questions, thank you.
Judge:	*(To Ent)* Thank you, you may step down.
	(Ent returns to his/her seat in the court room.)
	(To Prosecution) You may call your next witness.
Prosecution 2:	Thank you. We call the Wood Goblin to the stand.
	(The Wood Goblin enters the witness stand.)
Court Clerk:	*(Approaches the witness stand).* Do you swear to tell the truth, the whole truth, and nothing but the truth?
Wood Goblin:	I do.
Court Clerk:	State your name and address, please.
Wood Goblin:	I'm Willard/Wilma Wood Goblin, and I live in Stump Number 35, Storybook Forest.
Court Clerk:	Thank you. You may be seated.
	(The Wood Goblin sits down in the witness stand. The Court Clerk returns to his/her seat.)
Prosecution 2:	Mr./Ms. Wood Goblin, what are your responsibilities in the forest?
Wood Goblin:	I'm a refuse collection engineer.
Prosecution 2:	So, for the record, and to avoid any confusion, we will refer to you as an engineer. That is a very noble job – you must be very proud.
Wood Goblin:	Yeah, sure … can we get on with this? I got an appointment at "tree" o'clock!
Judge:	I must caution you, Mr./Ms. Wood Goblin. Please keep your comments to yourself.
Wood Goblin:	Yeah, yeah. Okay, My Lord/My Lady … sorry about that.
Prosecution 2:	How do you know Hansel and Gretel?
Wood Goblin:	I've been cleaning up after them for a while now. They've been dropping junk everywhere they go. First, I picked up shiny stones that don't belong in the forest, then I picked up bread crumbs that they threw all over the place.

Prosecution 2:	Are these some examples of the shiny rocks?
Wood Goblin:	Yes!
Prosecution 2:	Thank you. My Lord/My Lady, we would like to submit this as Exhibit 1.
	(The Court Clerk labels the bag of shiny rocks as Exhibit 1, then shows it to the Jury before showing it to the Judge.)
Prosecution 2:	And how did it make you feel to clean up after them?
Defence:	Objection, My Lord/My Lady. The Prosecution is playing on personal emotion!
Judge:	Overruled. Prosecution, please continue.
Prosecution 2:	And how did that make you feel?
Wood Goblin:	Fed up! I've got more important things to do – this week I've got a big oil spill to clean up as well as the usual piles of trash from campers!
Prosecution 2:	Ahhh … okay. In your journeys cleaning up after Hansel and Gretel, did you witness any other disturbing behavior?
Wood Goblin:	Only the murder of the witch, old Rosie Daintymouth. After my shift, I decided to go and give those kids a piece of my mind. I've known Rosina and Grizelda since I started this job and I knew that Rosie would understand. I decided against talking to the kids, though, when I saw them in Rosie's cottage, through the window, stuffing her headfirst into the furnace.
Prosecution 2:	You saw the murder as it happened?
Wood Goblin:	What did I just say? Yeah, I saw the murder!
Prosecution 2:	So, let me get this straight for the records, Mr./Ms. Wood Goblin. Are you saying that you saw this boy (points to Hansel) and this girl (points to Gretel) murder one Rosina Daintymouth, witch of the forest?
Defence 2	Objection to the word "murder." Conjecture on the part of the witness.
Judge:	Sustained. *(To Wood Goblin)* Just say what you saw, not what you assume.
Wood Goblin:	I saw them push Rosie into the oven! Can I go now? I've got ten kids waiting for me at home, and I was supposed to be there two hours ago! I'm not going to be home for another hour with this traffic!
Prosecution 2:	One more question, Mr./Ms. Wood Goblin. Did it come to your attention that Hansel and Gretel broke into the cottage of the witch? That they were uninvited guests?
Defence 2:	Objection. Hearsay.
Judge:	Sustained.
Prosecution 2:	Did you see Hansel and Gretel break in to the witch's cottage?

Wood Goblin:	Well I didn't see them break in. Maybe they walked right in without asking, but then maybe Rosina persuaded them in – who knows!
Prosecution 2:	Thank you. My Lord/My Lady, no further questions.
Judge:	Does Defence wish to cross-examine?
Defence 2:	Yes, My Lord/My Lady.
	Wood Goblin, how many rocks are in this forest?
Wood Goblin:	What am I – the municipal government? I don't have an inventory of every rock in this forest!
Defence 2:	Yet you found the time to pursue these shiny rocks for the entire length of your shift.
Wood Goblin:	Those rocks were way too shiny for that particular segment of the forest!
Defence 2:	How did you become an expert on rocks?
Prosecution 2:	Objection, My Lord/My Lady. Badgering the witness!
Judge:	Sustained. I caution the Defence – proceed.
Defence 2:	I am sorry, My Lord/My Lady. The Defence finds it hard to believe that shiny rocks could have such a negative effect on the forest. Let me try again. I find it interesting that Hansel and Gretel also had lots of rocks still with them when they were arrested.
Wood Goblin:	All I can say is that these humans should all be put away! I am sick and tired of cleaning up after them – the trash, the noise, and the big ugly footprints they leave!
Defence 2:	Can't we see how biased the Wood Goblin is?!
Judge:	That is up to the Jury to decide, Counsel.
Defence 2:	No further questions.
Prosecution 3:	Yes, My Lord/My Lady. Thank you. We call Grizelda Daintymouth to the stand.
	(Grizelda Daintymouth enters the witness stand.)
Court Clerk:	*(Approaches the witness stand).* Do you swear to tell the truth, the whole truth, and nothing but the truth?
Grizelda:	I do.
Court Clerk:	State your name and address, please
Grizelda:	I am Grizelda Daintymouth, witch of the forest, and I live in Spice Cottage, in Storybook Forest.
Court Clerk:	Thank you. You may be seated.

(Grizelda Daintymouth sits down in the witness stand. The Court Clerk returns to his/her seat.)

Prosecution 3: Walk me through what happened when you came home from your vacation at the end of July this year. Tell me what you witnessed when you entered your vandalized cottage.

Grizelda: I could already see apparent changes to the cottage from the gate. The chocolate windowsill had been bitten off, the lollipop doorknob was nowhere in sight, even the candy cane porch railing had been chewed up.

Prosecution 3: Is that so? Tell me about the interior of the cottage. What did you see?

Grizelda: Well, let me just put it this way ... I figured my sister threw another one of those Evil-ware parties and that it had got out of control. But my sister was nowhere in sight. I couldn't find her! Well, I had had a long flight and I was all broomed-out, so I figured I would start by baking the repair pieces for the cottage. I opened the oven door and to my horror and utter shock, there was my sister Rosina!

Prosecution 3: That must have been a traumatic experience for you! Did you have any idea who could have committed such a heinous act?

Grizelda: I figured that it was a couple of kids, since their small footprints were all over the cottage. They left a mess of chicken bones and flour, and the door of the cage we have in the comer for ... uh, for our, uh, pig was broken. The children had left a mess all over the place.

Prosecution 3: Have you cleaned up and replaced all of the broken articles on the inside and outside of the cottage?

Grizelda: Well, I have replaced the eaten candy, cakes, and chocolate, and the inside of the cottage is now clean, but my sister is dead, and no amount of cleaning or replacing can bring her back!

(She sobs noisily.)

Prosecution 3: Was there anything else missing from the cottage?

Grizelda: Yes, there was. My sister had large caskets of pearls, baskets of diamonds, and chests of treasure that she'd collected her whole life, from all over the world. These items were bequeathed to me in her will. Now that she is dead, I can no longer afford to keep my cottage of candy, because she paid the mortgage. I was supposed to sell her pearls, her diamonds, and the treasure, so I would have the money to live comfortably for the rest of my life. These are all gone. Now I shall become a pauper.

Prosecution 3: Thank you. My Lord/My Lady, no further questions.

Judge: Does Defence wish to cross-examine?

Defence 3: Yes, My Lord/My Lady.

Madam Daintymouth, why would you build a candy cottage?

Grizelda: Both my sister – may she rest in peace – and I love sweets, and we wanted to live out the remainder of our lives in a home that we enjoyed.

Defence 3: Isn't it true, Madam Daintymouth, that the two of you built the candy cottage to lure children, so that you could eat them?

Grizelda: WHAT? Why that is the most preposterous …

Prosecution 3: Objection! My Lord/My Lady, Defence is leading the witness!

Judge: Sustained – Defence, reword your question.

Defence 3: Sorry, My Lord/My Lady. Witch Daintymouth, what is your pig's name? And may I caution you that you are under oath.

Grizelda: Ummm …

Defence 3: Okay, let me stop you before you finish that statement. Police reports and inventories do not list the presence of any such pig, nor do they list the presence of any pig accessories or paraphernalia such as pig food. Truthfully, do you in fact own a pig?

Grizelda: … No, I don't …

Defence 3: You see, I would come to the conclusion, having overheard the rumors in the forest, that the cage you claim is intended for your pig is, in fact, not intended for livestock at all, but for small children. Is that true?

Grizelda: This is ridiculous – I am not the one on trial here!

Prosecution 3: Objection! Badgering the witness!

Judge: Overruled, but I advise the Defence to quickly come to the point of this questioning.

Defence 3: My point is this, My Lord/My Lady: the Defence would like to submit these strands of hair and correlating crime scene reports as Exhibits 2 and 3.

(He holds up a plastic bag containing strands of hair and a sheaf of papers to give to the Court Clerk.)

(The Court Clerk labels the plastic bag as "Exhibit 2" and the papers as "Exhibit 3, then shows them to the Jury before showing them to the Judge.)

These strands of hair, with follicles attached, are an exact DNA match to those of Hansel, and were found in Rosina and Grizelda Daintymouth's cage. The crime scene report states that none of Hansel's hair follicles were found anywhere else in the cottage. The report also states that the time elapsed in order for one human to shed that amount of hair naturally would be approximately four weeks.

Now tell me, have you ever consumed a child?

Grizelda:	*(Sobs quietly.)*
Defence 3:	I am going to take your silence as a yes. Would I be incorrect in my assumption?
Grizelda:	*(Sobs)* … No, you are not wrong.
Defence 3:	Thank you, My Lord/My Lady, no further questions.
Judge:	*(To Grizelda Daintymouth)* Thank you, you may step down.
	(Grizelda Daintymouth returns to her seat in the courtroom.)
	Does the Prosecution wish to call any further witnesses?
Prosecution 3:	No, My Lord/My Lady. We rest our case.
Judge:	*(To Prosecution)* Thank you.
	(To Defence) Defence's opening statement please.
Defence 1:	*(Opening statement.)* My Lord/My Lady, we intend to show that Hansel and Gretel have been wrongfully charged on all counts. Being left alone in the forest at such a young age is extremely frightening. Hansel and Gretel, left alone without any food, weapons, or way of fending for themselves, would surely have died. They had no intention of causing damage to the old witches' private property, but they were so over whelmed with hunger and relief at seeing any food – not to speak of a cottage built of candy – that they did what any young child would do – they ate.

My Lord/My Lady, as to the charge of breaking and entering, one cannot be charged when one is invited inside. We will prove to the court that the old witch Rosina had a motive for inviting the children in. Being trustful and naive, the children, filled with gratitude for their full bellies, unwittingly entered the candy cottage to undergo four weeks of torture and loneliness, and face impending death. The old witch's untimely death, My Lord/My Lady, was an act of self-defence on the part of Gretel, for they were told countless times that they would be killed and eaten.

After this traumatic experience and the death of the old witch Rosina, Hansel and Gretel found a large stash of riches. After having lived their whole lives in poverty, the children's young minds could only think of helping their family as best they could, by taking the riches that belonged to the old witch. At that point, too, it seemed only just that these jewels should be compensation for the imprisonment and abuse they had suffered.

To support our case, we will be calling Little Red Riding Hood, Hansel, and Gretel as witnesses.

We now call Little Red Riding Hood to the stand.

(Little Red Riding Hood enters the witness stand.)

Court Clerk:	*(Approaches the witness stand)* Do you swear to tell the truth, the whole truth, and nothing but the truth?
Red Riding Hood:	I do.
Court Clerk:	State your name and address, please.
Red Riding Hood:	I'm called Little Red Riding Hood, and I live in Rose Cottage, in Storybook Forest.
Court Clerk:	Thank you. You may be seated.
	(Little Red Riding Hood sits down in the witness stand. The Court Clerk returns to his/her seat.)
Defence 1:	Little Red Riding Hood, what do you do for employment?
Red Riding Hood:	Well, I have been delivering flowers, apples, and medicine to the elderly people of Storybook Forest for years.
Defence 1:	How did you begin such work?
Red Riding Hood:	When my grandmother was ill, my mother would send me to her house with flowers, baking, apples, preserves, and medicine to help my grand mother feel better. Eventually, I began visiting other elderly people in addition to my grandmother.
Defence 1:	When you travel from your home to the homes of the elderly, which route do you take?
Red Riding Hood:	I always take route 6, which is the path that crosses the Ent forest and cuts between the notorious candy cottage and the river.
Defence 1:	What do you mean by "notorious candy cottage"?
Red Riding Hood:	Everybody knows not to get too close to that horrible cottage because the witches inside will eat you!
Defence 1:	Have you had any personal experiences with the Daintymouth sisters yourself?
Red Riding Hood:	Yes. About two years ago, I was walking to the home of a client when one of the witches tried to entice me near their cottage with cotton candy. It's my favorite, so I went to her.
Defence 1:	And can you tell the court what happened?

Red Riding Hood:	Sure. I ate the cotton candy and started to feel really sleepy. The witch – I don't remember which witch is which – asked me if I wanted to go inside the cottage and take a nap. I was warned too many times by my mother to never, NEVER go inside, so I ran away. I curled up near a tree and slept it off. It took six hours for me to wake up! My mother was so worried.
Defence 1:	Have you had any other confrontations with either witch?
Red Riding Hood:	No, thank heavens!
Defence 1:	Have you heard any stories about children being kidnapped and eaten by the witches?
Prosecution 1:	Objection! Leading the witness and hearsay!
Defence 1:	My Lord/My Lady, I am merely attempting to establish the reputation of these sisters.
Judge:	Overruled. Continue your questioning.
Red Riding Hood:	Yes, here are stories that the witches eat children on a regular basis. There are "missing person" posters all over the place in Storybook City! It's scary! I think it's a miracle that I got away!
Prosecution 1:	Objection! Conjecture on the part of the witness.
Judge:	Sustained.
Defence 1:	You'll have to excuse me for bringing the following subject up. Please remember that you are not on trial here, but isn't it true that you were charged with possession of an illegal weapon on the 23rd of October, 20~~?
Red Riding Hood:	Well, yes, but …
Defence 1:	Why did you need an illegal weapon?
Red Riding Hood:	Well, I didn't want to pass that cottage without one!
Defence 1:	Thank you, My Lord/My Lady, no further questions.
Judge:	Does Prosecution wish to cross-examine?
Prosecution 1:	Yes, My Lord/My Lady.
	Little Red Riding Hood, why do you use route #6 if you are so afraid of the area in which the witches live?
Red Riding Hood:	It is an easier walk, and it doesn't take as much time as the highway.
Prosecution 1:	Wouldn't your safety be more important to you than the little extra time and energy it would take to walk to your clients' homes by another route?
Red Riding Hood:	The only bad part about route 6 is the candy cottage – that is what makes the walk scary! The people of Storybook Forest are very kind and caring and always look out for one another – except for the witches.

Prosecution 1:	Is it not true that you were expelled from witch school?
Red Riding Hood:	Well, yes, but I …
Prosecution 1:	It seems to me that you have a motive to put these witches away!
Defence 1:	Objection!
Judge:	Sustained.
Prosecution 1:	Thank you, My Lord/My Lady, no further questions.
Judge:	*(To Little Red Riding Hood)* Thank you, you may step down.
	(Little Red Riding Hood returns to her seat in the courtroom.)
	(To Defence) You may call your next witness.
Defence 2:	Thank you. We call Hansel to the stand.
	(Hansel enters the witness stand. Sheriff 1 accompanies Hansel to the stand.)
Court Clerk:	*(Approaches the witness stand)* Do you swear to tell the truth, the whole truth, and nothing but the truth?
Hansel:	I do.
Court Clerk:	State your name and address, please.
Hansel:	My name is Hansel, and I live at Twelve Oaks Estate, in Storybook Forest.
Court Clerk:	Thank you. You may be seated.
	(Hansel sits down in the witness stand. The Court Clerk returns to his/her seat.)
Defence 2:	Hansel, I want you to walk me through your experiences in the cottage, starting with the first day you met the witch Rosina Daintymouth in June, as best you can.
Hansel:	I was walking with my sister through the forest in a panic, we were so very hungry. All I wanted was a piece of bread, or anything to eat to get me by. Then a miracle happened. I thought that it was a mirage! I couldn't believe my eyes – there in front of us, in the distance, was a cottage built of candy!
Defence 2:	Go on, Hansel, you're doing great!
Hansel:	Nothing could have stopped me from tearing into that cottage, though I was glad when this charming old lady told us to feel free to eat any part of the house. I was so comforted, she seemed like the grandmother that I never had. She was so concerned with our health. I remember her saying to us, "Don't eat too much or you will get sick!" Well, I ate my fill and to tell you the truth, I was getting a little bit sleepy. It was getting dark, and I couldn't believe my ears when she invited us inside to spend

the night. Gretel and I agreed because we were both so exhausted from wandering around the forest.

Defence 2:	Then what happened?
Hansel:	In the middle of the night I … (sobs)
Defence 2:	Take your time, you are safe now …
Prosecution:	Objection, My Lord/My Lady! Playing on emotion!
Defence 2:	My Lord/My Lady, Hansel has obviously undergone a very traumatic experience. Will the court deny him his humanity?
Judge:	Overruled. You may continue.
Defence 2:	Please, Hansel, if you would …
Hansel:	In the middle of the night, I woke up to these claws; they were like talons … ripping me out of bed. Before I was even awake, I found myself in a cage, locked up like an animal!
Defence 2:	What was happening to Gretel at this time?
Hansel:	I'm sorry, but I don't remember. I was still trying to understand what was happening to me. The witch started cackling about eating me – I was terrified!
Defence 2:	How long were you in the cage?
Hansel:	Could have been days, weeks, or months. I don't know – it was all a blur and time meant nothing to me. I would eat when I was fed and sleep as much as possible.
Defence 2:	You are lucky to be alive. Do you have traumatic stress syndrome for the trauma that you endured?
Hansel:	Well I'm very upset, if that's what you mean.
Defence 2:	And what do your doctors say?
Prosecution 2:	Objection! Hearsay!
Judge:	Sustained. Defence, change your line of questioning.
Defence 2:	Yes, My Lord/My Lady. Hansel, will you ever go near that cottage again?
Hansel:	Never. No question EVER! (Sobs.)
Defence 2:	Thank you, My Lord/My Lady, no further questions.
Judge:	Does Prosecution wish to cross-examine?
Prosecution 2:	Yes, My Lord/My Lady.
	Hansel, why did you really leave the safety of your parents' home?
Hansel:	What do you mean?
Prosecution 2:	I am willing to jump to the conclusion that you and your sister left your parents' home to cause havoc, vandalism, and other delinquent crimes

	… like theft and murder.
Defence 2:	Objection! Jumping to conclusion!
Judge:	Sustained. Get to your point.
Prosecution 2:	Did you take anything out of Rosina and Grizelda Daintymouth's cottage that did not belong to you?
Hansel:	Well, a few little things …
Prosecution 2:	I would say that you took more than a "few little things." The Prosecution would like to submit Exhibit 4, a notarized inventory of all the diamonds, pearls, and treasure owned by the late Rosina Daintymouth. Crime scene reports show no sign of these jewels. Did you take them?
Hansel:	She had me locked up like an animal for FOUR WEEKS! I deserved those jewels!
Prosecution 2:	That has yet to be proven. Until then, those jewels belong to Grizelda Daintymouth, and you have just admitted to the theft. Thank you, My Lord/My Lady, no further questions.
Judge:	*(To Hansel)* Thank you, you may step down.
	(Hansel returns to his seat in the courtroom, followed by Sheriff 1.)
	(To Defence) You may call your next witness.
Defence 3:	Thank you. We call Gretel to the stand.
Court Clerk:	*(Approaches the witness stand. Sheriff 1 accompanies her to the stand.)* Do you swear to tell the truth, the whole truth, and nothing but the truth?
Gretel:	I do.
Court Clerk:	Please state your name and address.
Gretel:	My name is Gretel, and I live at Twelve Oaks Estate, in Storybook Forest.
Court Clerk:	Thank you. You may be seated.
	(Gretel sits down in the witness stand. The Court Clerk returns to his/her seat.)
Defence 3:	Gretel, how old are you?
Gretel:	I am ~~ years old.
Defence 3:	You will have to pardon my saying so, but you look much older than ~~. I guess four weeks of hard labor will do that to a person!
Prosecution 3:	Objection! The Defence is performing for the Jury!
Judge:	Sustained. Defence, I will not warn you again!

Defence 3:	Gretel, I'm going to ask you this question up front. I don't want to play any games with you, or attempt to pull the proverbial wool over the Jury's eyes. Did you kill the witch?
Gretel:	…Yes, I did …
Defence 3:	Did you have any preconceived notion to do so, or were you simply reacting to circumstances as they occurred?
Gretel:	(Sobs) It was either her or Hansel and I. It had been four weeks and I had had enough, a person can only take so much candy!
Defence 3:	Calm down, Gretel, take a deep breath … you are not alone in your grief …
Prosecution 3:	(Loudly) OH! Give me a break …
Judge:	Prosecution? Did you have something to add? Shall I remind you about court etiquette? I didn't think so.
	Please, continue, Gretel.
Gretel:	I tricked her into getting close to the furnace. Close enough so that I could push her into it … and then I did it. For a split second, I do admit, I enjoyed it! It was finally freedom! (Sobs louder.)
Defence 3:	I have no doubt that the Prosecution will attempt to make your action seem as though it had malicious intent, but considering the intense circumstances that you endured for four terrible weeks, you and I both know that it was in fact self-defence. Is this true?
Gretel:	(Sobs) Oh yes, absolutely. I am not a murderer.
Defence 3:	Thank you, Gretel. My Lord/My Lady, no further questions.
Judge:	Does Prosecution wish to cross examine?
Prosecution 3:	Yes, My Lord/My Lady.
	Gretel, that was a terrific performance. Can you explain to me why, in my many years of practice, I have never encountered a witness under oath who admitted to enjoying the so-called "freedom" that was in fact the brutal slaughter of an elderly, near-blind woman?
Gretel:	That is not what I …
Prosecution 3:	In my experience, in the field of law, the only person who would openly admit to enjoying a murder for any reason would be a confessed killer. Do you wish, at this time, to confess your guilt?
Defence 3:	Objection! Badgering the witness!
Judge:	Sustained. Ask your question in a different way.
Prosecution 3:	Did you murder Rosina?
Gretel:	(Sobs) I am not a murderer!

Prosecution 3:	Thank you, My Lord/My Lady, no further questions.
Judge:	*(To Gretel)* Thank you, you may step down.
	(Gretel returns to her seat in the courtroom, followed by Sheriff 1.)
	Does the Defence wish to call any further witnesses?
Defence 3:	No, My Lord/My Lady. We rest our case.
Judge:	Thank you. You may now give your closing statement to the Jury.
Defence 1:	*(Closing statement)* Ladies and gentlemen of the Jury … you know, when we are tired, we do not think too well. Put me in rush hour traffic and my IQ drops 20 points. Put yourselves in the place of Hansel and Gretel – exhausted, hungry, lost, lonely, and young. Imagine being all of these things and suddenly coming across a house made of all of your favorite foods. Imagine a charming old lady who reminds you of what a grandmother should be, inviting you to eat any part of this giant goody house. It seems too good to be true, doesn't it? That's because it is!

The only thing that these children are guilty of is naïveté and the lack of sufficient common sense to realize that they had fallen victim to a predator. Now, what will prey do to escape its predator? What will prey do to save its own life? Everything possible! Ladies and gentlemen of the Jury, you too would do anything to save your own life and the lives of those dearest to you, would you not? These children did, and unfortunately that led to the demise of a not-so-charming witch. As for the jewels, the witch always said: take what you can in this house and eat and eat! So they did!

I thank you for your time, thank you in advance for making the right decision, and thank you for using this court as a vehicle of the good and righteous.

Judge:	*(To Defence)* Thank you.
	(To Prosecution) You may now give your closing statement to the Jury.
Prosecution 1:	*(Closing statement)* Ladies and gentle men of the Jury, I am counsel for the Prosecution. A Prosecutor does not achieve this position after four years at a second-rate law school. I have many years' experience. I have, as they say, been around the block. I have seen many defence mechanisms in my day. These Hollywood-style tactics do not fool me, and I know very well that they do not fool

you either. The scales of justice will not be balanced by scripted tears and sobs. What we have here is a classic Jury swinging defence which attempts to tug at your heartstrings.

Here are the facts: A woman is dead, brutally murdered. Jewels are missing from the victim's damaged cottage, and two children are putting on award-winning performances in order to try and save themselves from justice. I hope with all of my heart that you see what it is that I see – because what I see are two littering pyromaniacs who thrill in vandalism, breaking and entering, theft, and finally the brutal slayings of the elderly. I implore you, ladies and gentlemen of the Jury, do not allow   these young criminals to grow up living in the freedom of which they deprived Rosina Daintymouth, to sharpen their skills as criminals of the highest calibre. We ask that you find Hansel and Gretel guilty of all charges laid against them! Thank you.

Judge:

(To Prosecution) Thank you.

(Judge's charge to the Jury) As members of the Jury, you will have to make a decision of whether Hansel   and Gretel are guilty or not guilty for each charge.

Hansel and Gretel stand charged that they:

"Did commit mischief by willfully damaging property belonging to the witch Rosina Daintymouth, contrary to section 430(1) of *The Criminal Code of Canada.*

"Did commit break and enter of the witch Rosina Daintymouth's residence, with intent to commit an indictable offence therein, contrary to section 348(1)(a) of the Criminal Code of Canada.

"Did commit the murder of the witch Rosina Daintymouth, contrary to section 229 of *The Criminal Code of Canada.*

"Did commit theft over $5 000 of pearls and precious stones belonging to the witch Rosina Daintymouth, contrary to section 334(a) of *The Criminal Code of Canada.*

Think about what the witnesses and lawyers said during the trial. Your job is to carefully weigh the evidence from the both the prosecution and defence witnesses and lawyers and come to a decision. You need to decide which witnesses are more believable and which argument is most plausible. You will then vote on each charge. For this trial, your Jury is only required to reach a majority decision.

You now have 15 minutes to discuss the case. When you return, I will ask your foreperson your verdict.

This is a suggested script only. Judges can feel free to elaborate.

Sheriff 2:	Order in the court. All rise.
	(Everyone stands.)
Court Clerk:	Court will now adjourn for 15 minutes.
	The Jury leaves the courtroom to discuss the trial.
	(When the Jury are ready to return, approximately 15 minutes later, Sheriff 2 calls the court to order.)

Sheriff 2:	Order in the court. All rise.
	(Everyone stands as the Jury and then the Judge enter the courtroom and are seated.)
Jury	*(All participants sit.)*
Judge:	Mr./Madam Foreperson, have you reached a verdict?
Foreperson:	*(Stands)* Yes, My Lord/My Lady.
Court Clerk:	*(Stands)* Will the defendants please rise?
	(Hansel and Gretel and Sheriff 1 all stand.)
Judge:	*(To Foreperson)* You may read the verdict.
Foreperson:	We find the accused, Hansel and Gretel, guilty/not guilty of the charge of mischief by wilfully damaging the property of Rosina Daintymouth, guilty/not guilty of the charge of break and enter Rosina Daintymouth's residence, guilty/not guilty of the murder of Rosina Daintymouth, and guilty/not guilty of theft of valuables belonging to Rosina Daintymouth.
Judge:	Thank you.
	(The Judge then passes sentence if Hansel and Gretel are found guilty of any of the charges, or acquits Hansel and Gretel if they are found not guilty of all charges.)
Sheriff 1:	*(Standing)* Order in the court. All rise.
	(All participants stand.)
Court Clerk:	This court is now adjourned.

Alice in Wonderland Mock Trial

Her Majesty the Queen v. Alice

By Heather Gascoigne

Recommended for Grades 4 to 7

Case for the Prosecution

That Alice did commit the crimes of disturbing the peace in Wonderland by fighting and shouting in the Queen of Hearts' rose garden, and also did commit theft under $5 000 of a box of currant cookies belonging to the White Rabbit.

Case for the Defence

That Alice did not intentionally cause a disturbance in Wonderland. She was upset and confused because she was lost and was continually changing size. In spite of her traumatic experiences, Alice tried to be helpful in her encounters with Wonderland residents and always asked for directions politely. She ate the White Rabbit's currant cookies because she was very tired and hungry, and also because she was hoping that they would shrink her back to her proper size so she could leave the White Rabbit's cottage.

Trial Roles

Judge (best played by an adult)

Prosecution Lawyers 1, 2, and 3
Defence Lawyers 1, 2, and 3

Prosecution Witnesses:
Knave of Hearts
White Rabbit
Queen of Hearts

Defence Witnesses:
Alice
Cheshire Cat
Mad Hatter

Officers of the Court:
Court Clerk
Court Reporter
Sheriffs 1 and 2

Members of the Jury, one of whom is appointed Foreperson

Members of the Media:
Print journalists
Television reporters
Court Artist

Suggestions for Costumes, Props, and Exhibits

Costumes

Judge	Gown
Prosecution Lawyers	Black gowns
Defence Lawyers	Black gowns
Court Clerk	Black gown
Court Reporter	Black gown
Sheriffs 1 and 2	Brown hats and jackets
Knave of Hearts	Sandwich board/tunic decorated as a Jack of Hearts playing card, red tights
White Rabbit	Rabbit costume, waistcoat, checked jacket, and pocket watch; could carry white gloves and a large fan
Queen of Hearts	Robe with hearts printed on it, crown; could carry a sceptre topped with a heart
Alice	Dress with sash and apron, hair band
Cheshire Cat	Cat costume, face painted with a large grin
Mad Hatter	Jacket, large bow tie, hat with a large price tag pinned to it
Court Artist	Smock and beret; could carry paper and coloring pencils
Members of the Media	Name tags or press identification attached to hats or jackets, or worn around the neck; could carry pens, notebooks, and camera
Members of the Jury	Playing card soldiers: waist-long sandwich boards decorated as playing cards, black or red tights

Props

Indictment (a sheet of paper on which the charge is written)

Exhibits

Exhibit 1:	Fingerprint charts
Exhibit 2:	Empty cookie box
Exhibit 3:	Bottle labelled "Drink Me"

Procedure

Entering the Courtroom

1. The teacher welcomes the guests and reviews the intent and format of the trial, and the role of the audience.
2. The Prosecution and Defence lawyers arrive and sit at their tables.
3. The witnesses and media arrive and sit in the areas reserved for them.
4. Sheriff 1 enters the courtroom with Alice. He/she seats Alice in the prisoner's box and sits nearby.

5. The Court Clerk and Court Reporter arrive and take their places.

6. Sheriff 2 calls the court to order, and asks everyone to stand.

7. The Judge and Jury enter the courtroom with Sheriff 2 and take their places. After the Judge and Jury are seated, the public sits down and the trial is ready to begin.

Trial Procedure

1. The Court Clerk reads out the indictment.

2. The Prosecution and Defence lawyers introduce themselves to the Judge.

3. Prosecution makes an opening statement to the Jury, presenting what they intend to prove and listing their witnesses: the Knave of Hearts, the White Rabbit, and the Queen of Hearts.

4. Prosecution calls the Knave of Hearts to the stand.

5. Defence cross-examines the Knave of Hearts.

6. Prosecution calls the Queen of Hearts to the stand.

7. Defence cross-examines the Queen of Hearts.

8. Prosecution calls the White Rabbit to the stand.

9. Defence chooses not to cross-examine the White Rabbit.

10. Prosecution rises and says to the Judge that the Prosecution's case is concluded.

11. Defence makes a short opening statement to the Jury, outlining their defence and listing their witnesses: Alice, the Cheshire Cat, and the Mad Hatter.

12. Defence calls Alice to the stand.

13. Prosecution cross-examines Alice.

14. Defence calls the Cheshire Cat to the stand.

15. Prosecution chooses not to cross-examine the Cheshire Cat.

16. Defence calls the Mad Hatter to the stand.

17. Prosecution cross-examines the Mad Hatter.

18. Defence rises and says to the Judge that the Defence case is concluded.

19. Defence makes a closing statement to the Judge and Jury.

20. Prosecution makes a closing statement to the Judge and Jury.

21. The Judge makes a brief statement to the Jury, reviewing the charges and instructs them to go to the Jury room to decide their verdict.

22. Sheriff 2 says "Order in the court. All rise."

22. The Judge and the Jury exit the courtroom.

23. The Jury discusses the trial.

24. Sheriff 2 says "Order in the court. All rise."

25. The Jury and Judge return, accompanied by Sheriff 2.

26. The Judge asks the Jury for the verdict.

27. The Foreperson reads out the verdict of guilty or not guilty for each charge. If Alice is found guilty of either charge, the Judge will impose an appropriate sentence. Otherwise, the Judge tells Alice she is free to go.

28. The Court Clerk adjourns the court.

Trial Script

Sheriff 2:	Order in the court. All rise.
	(Everyone stands as the Jury and then the Judge enter the courtroom with Sheriff 2 accompanying them.)
Court Clerk:	This court is now in session. Mr./Madam Justice ~~~ presiding.
Judge:	You may be seated.
	(All participants sit. Sheriff 1 is seated by Alice. Sheriff 2 sits between the Judge and Jury.)
	Are all parties present?
Prosecution 1:	*(Stands and addresses the Judge)* Yes, My Lord/My Lady. In the case of Her Majesty the Queen against Alice, I am _____, and with me are _____ and _____, acting on behalf of the Prosecution.
	(Each member of the Prosecution stands as he/she is introduced; all sit after introductions are finished.)
Defence 1:	*(Stands and addresses the Judge)* My Lord/My Lady, I am _____, and with me are _____ and _____, acting on behalf of the accused, Alice.
	(Each member of the Defence stands as he/she is introduced; all sit after introductions are finished.)
Judge:	Thank you.
	(To Court Clerk) Please read the charge.
Court Clerk:	Will the defendant please rise?
	(Alice and Sheriff 1 stand.)
Court Clerk:	*(Reading from the indictment)* Alice, you stand charged that on or about April 1st, 20~~, at Wonderland, in the Province/Territory of ~~~, you did cause a disturbance in or near a public place, namely the Queen of Hearts' garden, by fighting and shouting, contrary to section 175(1)(a) of *The Criminal Code of Canada*. How do you plead?
Alice:	Not guilty, My Lord/My Lady.
Court Clerk:	Alice, you stand charged that on or about April 1st, 20~~, at Wonderland, in the Province/Territory of ~~~, you did steal a box of currant cookies, the property of the White Rabbit, of a value not exceeding $5 000, contrary to section 334(b) of *The Criminal Code of Canada*. How do you plead?
Alice:	Not guilty, My Lord/My Lady.
Court Clerk:	My Lord/My Lady, the accused pleads not guilty to both charges.
Judge:	Thank you. You may be seated.

(Those standing now sit down.)

(To Prosecution) Please proceed with your case.

Prosecution: *(Opening statement)* My Lord/My Lady, we intend to prove that after Alice followed the White Rabbit down the rabbit hole into Wonderland, a place where she had no right to be, she created a disturbance in the Queen of Hearts' garden. This was only one of the many disruptions she caused in the lives of the residents of Wonderland: she annoyed people with her many requests for directions, her incessant questions, and, of course, her habit of continually changing size. Furthermore, she helped herself to food and drink which wasn't hers, and interrupted a tea party and a croquet game to which she hadn't been invited.

To support our case, we will be calling the Knave of Hearts, who was the officer who arrested Alice, the White Rabbit, and the Queen of Hearts. We now wish to call the Knave of Hearts.

(The Knave of Hearts enters the witness stand. Usually, all witnesses remain standing only until they have been sworn in, but the Knave of Hearts, as the arresting officer, remains standing throughout his/her testimony.)

Court Clerk: *(Approaches the witness stand)* Do you swear to tell the truth, the whole truth, and nothing but the truth?

Knave of Hearts: I do.

Court Clerk: State your name and address, please.

Knave of Hearts: I am the Knave of Hearts, and I live in Card Castle, in Wonderland.

Court Clerk: Thank you.

(The Court Clerk returns to his/her seat.)

Prosecution: Knave of Hearts, please tell the court what happened on April 1st of this year.

Knave of Hearts: The Queen of Hearts was giving her weekly croquet party in the castle rose garden. There was a disturbance, and she ordered me to break it up.

Prosecution: What did you find when you went to investigate this disturbance?

Knave:	There was a young girl pushing over the Queen's soldiers and yelling, "You're nothing but a pack of cards!" The flamingo mallets and the hedgehog balls were scampering all over the field, and the game was in ruin.
Prosecution:	Do you see that same little girl in the courtroom today?
Knave of Hearts:	Yes, that's her! (He points to Alice.)
Prosecution:	Let the record show that the witness, the Knave of Hearts, has identified the defendant Alice as the girl in question.
Prosecution:	What happened next?
Knave of Hearts:	The Queen was very angry. She is used to winning every game. She was yelling, "Off with her head!" So I arrested Alice and put her in the castle tower.
Prosecution:	Did you find any evidence at the scene?
Knave of Hearts:	Yes. I took her finger prints, and they matched ones I found on the cards which had been knocked over.
Prosecution:	Are these the finger print charts? (Shows the fingerprint charts to the Knave of Hearts.)
Knave of Hearts:	Yes, they have my signature on them.
Prosecution:	Court Clerk, please enter these charts as Exhibit 1.
	(The Court Clerk takes the charts, labels them "Exhibit 1," then shows them to the Jury before showing them to the Judge.)
	Thank you. No further questions, My Lord/My Lady.
Judge:	*(To Defence)* Do you wish to cross-examine this witness?
Defence:	*(Stands)* Yes, My Lord/My Lady.
	Knave of Hearts, were you present when this so-called disturbance started?
Knave of Hearts:	No, I was in the castle.
Defence:	Why were you in the castle when an important croquet game was being played?

Knave of Hearts:	I was locking up three gardeners who had been caught painting the roses red. The Queen was very angry with them. I didn't notice the disturbance until I returned.
Defence:	So, you did not actually see Alice start the disturbance?
Knave of Hearts:	Well, no.
Defence:	In fact, I suggest that it was really you who started the disturbance! You had slipped away to steal the jam tarts which the Queen of Hearts had made to have with tea after the game!
Prosecution:	*(Jumps up, speaking angrily)* My Lord/My Lady! I object! The Knave is not on trial – Alice is!
Judge:	Objection overruled, but I caution the Defence not to badger the witness. Witness, do you have anything to say? *(The Judge may make further comments if he or she wishes.)*
Knave of Hearts:	I deny that I caused any such disturbance!
Defence:	I have no further questions, My Lord/My Lady.
Judge:	*(To Knave of Hearts)* You may step down. (To Prosecution) You may call your next witness.
Prosecution 2:	We call the Queen of Hearts, My Lord/My Lady. *(The Queen of Hearts enters the witness stand.)*
Court Clerk:	*(Approaches the witness stand)* Do you swear to tell the truth, the whole truth, and nothing but the truth?
Queen of Hearts:	I do.
Court Clerk:	State your name and address, please.
Queen of Hearts:	*(Haughtily)* I am the Queen of Hearts, and I live in Card Castle, in Wonderland.
Court Clerk:	Thank you. You may be seated. *(The Queen of Hearts sits down in the witness stand. The Court Clerk returns to his/her seat.)*
Prosecution 2:	Queen of Hearts, who usually attends your weekly croquet parties?

Queen of Hearts:	Each week I have the White Rabbit deliver special invitations to a number of lucky citizens of Wonderland.
Prosecution 2:	And had you invited Alice to this week's game?
Queen of Hearts:	I most certainly had not! I'd never seen her before. She not only burst in on my croquet game uninvited, why, she did not even have the good manners to let me win!
Prosecution 2:	How did the disturbance start?
Queen of Hearts:	Alice could not seem to control her flamingo mallet and hedgehog ball. Everyone was getting all mixed up, and she had the nerve to keep asking what the rules were! Well! When she wouldn't even let me win, I finally shouted, "Off with her head!" and my soldiers surrounded her.
Prosecution 2:	Did she leave peacefully?
Queen of Hearts:	No! She started shouting, "You're nothing but a pack of cards!" and pushing my soldiers down to the ground, so my Knave of Hearts arrested her and took her to the castle tower.
Prosecution 2:	Thank you. No further questions, My Lord/My Lady.
Judge:	*(To Defence)* Do you wish to cross-examine this witness?
Defence 2:	Yes, My Lord/My Lady.
	Queen of Hearts, do you win every croquet game?
Queen of Hearts:	Of course.
Defence 2:	Was it surprising that a little girl would get overexcited and confused playing a game that had no rules?
Queen of Hearts:	Everyone else in Wonderland can do it.
Defence 2:	Don't you think that yelling "Off with her head!" and locking Alice in the tower was rather drastic?
Queen of Hearts:	No! Especially since no one had invited her in the first place!
Defence 2:	No further questions, My Lord/My Lady.
Judge:	*(To Queen of Hearts)* You may step down.

	(To Prosecution) You may call your last witness.
Prosecution 3:	We call the White Rabbit, My Lord/My Lady.
	(The White Rabbit enters the witness stand.)
Court Clerk:	*(Approaches the witness stand)* Do you swear to tell the truth, the whole truth, and nothing but the truth?
White Rabbit:	I do.
Court Clerk:	State your name and address, please.
White Rabbit:	White Rabbit, of Cosy Cottage, Wonderland.
Court Clerk:	You may be seated.
	(The White Rabbit sits down in the witness stand. The Court Clerk returns to his/her seat.)
Prosecution 3:	Where were you going on April 1st, 20~~ when you disappeared down the rabbit hole?
White Rabbit:	I was late for a very important date. I had forgotten my white gloves and fan, and was rushing home to get them before going to the Queen's croquet party.
Prosecution 3:	What happened when you noticed that Alice had followed you into Wonderland? Did you stop to speak to her?
White Rabbit:	*(Shocked)* Oh, my fuzzy ears and whiskers! No!
Prosecution 3:	What did she do then?
White Rabbit:	Well! It was very annoying! She followed me through Wonderland, upsetting the little mice and birds by talking about her cat, Dinah. Then she got mixed up in a caucus-race and complained because it had no beginning or end. She also frightened the flowers, who thought she was a weed.
Prosecution 3:	What happened when she finally caught up with you at your cottage?
White Rabbit:	She offered to go inside and run upstairs to my bedroom to get my white gloves and fan.
Prosecution 3:	And is that what she did?

White Rabbit:	No! She found a hidden box of very special cookies which I was saving for a special occasion, and ate them all up!
Prosecution 3:	*(Holding up a plastic bag containing a cookie box)* Is this the box that the cookies were in?
White Rabbit:	Yes.
Prosecution 3:	My Lord/My Lady, we would like to have this cookie box, which has Alice's fingerprints on it, entered as Exhibit 2.
	(He hands the box to the Court Clerk. The Court Clerk labels the plastic bag "Exhibit 2," then shows it to the Jury before showing it to the Judge.)
	(Prosecution turns back to the White Rabbit) Would you tell the court what happened when Alice ate the cookies?
White Rabbit:	She grew so big that her head pushed up the thatched roof of my cottage, and she had to dangle her arms out of the bedroom windows. Her hands reached into my garden!
Prosecution 3:	How did you get her out?
White Rabbit:	Well, she pulled a carrot out of the garden and nibbled on it. Then she became her normal size again, and ran down the stairs, out the door, and into the forest, without even saying she was sorry!
Prosecution 3:	Did you follow her?
White Rabbit:	Good gracious, no!
Prosecution 3:	When was the next time you saw her?
White Rabbit:	In the middle of a disturbance on the Queen of Hearts' croquet field.
Prosecution 3:	Thank you. No further questions, My Lord/My Lady.
Judge:	Does the Defence wish to cross-examine this witness?
Defence 3:	No, My Lord/My Lady.
Judge:	*(To White Rabbit)* You may step down.
	(The White Rabbit returns to his/her seat in the courtroom.)
Prosecution 3:	We rest our case, My Lord/My Lady.

Judge:	*(To Prosecution)* Thank you.
	(To Defence) The Defence may begin its case.
Defence 1:	*(Opening statement)* We submit that this little girl, Alice, has been wrongfully accused of both crimes. She followed the White Rabbit down the rabbit hole only because she was curious. She did not mean to upset the citizens of Wonderland and joined in their games and parties simply to be friendly.
	We will call Alice, the Cheshire Cat, and the Mad Hatter as witnesses. I now call the accused, Alice, to the stand.
	(Alice enters the witness stand. Sheriff 1 follows Alice and stands nearby.)
Court Clerk:	*(Approaches the witness stand)* Do you swear to tell the truth, the whole truth, and nothing but the truth?
Alice:	I do.
Court Clerk:	State your name and address, please.
Alice:	Alice. I live at 111 Curiosity Lane, Looking Glass Village.
Court Clerk:	You may be seated.
Defence 1:	Alice, what were you doing on the afternoon of April 1st, 20~~?
Alice:	I was sitting under a big oak tree in my yard with my cat Dinah, making a chain of spring flowers.
Defence 1:	What did you see while you were sitting there?
Alice:	A strange sight! It was very curious! A large white rabbit ran by.
Defence 1:	Can you describe this rabbit?
Alice:	Yes. He had white gloves, a fan, and the biggest gold watch I have ever seen on the end of a chain attached to his waistcoat.
Defence 1:	Did he say anything?
Alice:	Not to me, but he was muttering something about being late for a very important date!
Defence 1:	What happened next?
Alice:	He disappeared down a large rabbit hole under the hedge, and I was so curious I followed him.
Defence 1:	Did you find him?

Alice:	No! We fell down a long tunnel and he disappeared again, through a tiny door. It was too small for me to enter, but then I found a bottle which was labelled "Drink Me." When I did, I became small enough to get through the door.
Defence!:	Should you have drunk from the bottle, Alice?
Alice:	Perhaps it would have been wiser not to, but I didn't think I'd come to any harm, and I was so curious! Besides, why would the bottle say "Drink Me," if it wasn't supposed to be drunk?
Defence 1:	*(Holding up a bottle)* Is this the same bottle?
Alice:	It looks like it – it has the same label.
Defence 1:	My Lord/My Lady, we would like to have this bottle entered as Exhibit 3.
	(He hands the bottle to the Court Clerk. The Court Clerk labels the bottle "Exhibit 3," then shows it to the Jury before showing it to the Judge.)
	(Turning to Alice) Now, Alice, did you intend to bother the citizens of Wonderland?
Alice:	No. I was only asking directions and trying to find the White Rabbit. I'm sorry I scared the mice and birds and flowers, and spoiled the caucus-race. If only someone would have told me the rules.
Defence 1:	You've heard the testimony of the White Rabbit. Did you intend to grow so large, or to push his thatched roof off?
Alice:	No. I went upstairs only to get his white gloves and fan. I was just trying to be helpful.
Defence 1:	And did you intend to eat his special box of currant cookies?
Alice:	No, but there they were in the room, and I was beginning to get so tired and hungry from wandering all over Wonderland! But I did also wonder if those cookies might shrink me enough to leave the White Rabbit's house, which I thought would improve the situation for everyone. And that's what happened!
Defence 1:	Why did you run away without apologizing to the White Rabbit?
Alice:	I meant to, but I thought he'd be angry with me.
Defence 1:	What happened next?
Alice:	I met a Cheshire Cat, who had the biggest grin I have ever seen. He gave me directions to the home of the March Hare, a very close relation to the White Rabbit.
Defence 1:	Did the March Hare tell you which way to go?
Alice:	No. He was too busy having a tea party.
Defence 1:	Where did you finally find the White Rabbit?

Alice:	I wandered down a path and found myself in a lovely rose garden. The Queen of Hearts passed by with an escort of card soldiers, on her way to play croquet. Much to my surprise, the White Rabbit was also there, as he had been invited to play croquet with the Queen.
Defence 1:	In your own words, Alice, tell us what happened at the croquet game.
Alice:	Well, it was very strange. They used flamingos for mallets and hedgehogs for balls. There didn't seem to be any rules, as long as the Queen won.
Defence 1:	Did you intend to cause a disturbance?
Alice:	No. But my flamingo and hedgehog got away, and the Queen got angry. All of a sudden I was surrounded by a pack of card soldiers!
Defence 1:	What did you do?
Alice:	I tried to push them away, but the Knave of Hearts took me to the castle and locked me in the tower!
Defence 1:	Thank you, Alice. No further questions, My Lord/My Lady.
Judge:	Does the Prosecution wish to cross-examine this witness?
Prosecution 1:	Yes, My Lord/My Lady.
	Alice, don't you agree that if you hadn't been so curious and followed the White Rabbit into Wonderland, none of this would have happened?
Alice:	*(Sadly)* I try not to be curious. I give myself very good advice, but I very seldom follow it.
Prosecution 1:	No further questions, My Lord/My Lady.
Judge:	*(To Alice)* You may step down.
	(Alice steps down from the witness stand and returns to her seat, accompanied by Sheriff 1.)
	(To Defence) You may call your next witness.
	(Alice returns to her seat in the courtroom.)
Defence 2:	We call the Cheshire Cat, My Lord/My Lady.
	(The Cheshire Cat enters the witness stand.)
Court Clerk:	*(Approaches the witness stand)* Do you swear to tell the truth, the whole truth, and nothing but the truth?
Cheshire Cat:	I do.

Court Clerk:	State your name and address.
Cheshire Cat:	Cheshire Cat, Grinning Grove, Wonderland.
Court Clerk:	Thank you. You may be seated.
	(The Cheshire Cat sits down in the witness stand. The Court Clerk returns to his/her seat.)
Defence 2:	Do you know the defendant Alice?
Cheshire Cat:	I met her near the wood in Wonderland, on April 1st.
Defence 2:	What was she doing?
Cheshire Cat:	She was wandering about, looking for the White Rabbit, and asking for directions.
Defence 2:	What did she say to you?
Cheshire Cat:	She was very polite and asked which way she should go.
Defence 2:	And what was your answer?
Cheshire Cat:	I asked her where she wanted to go. She didn't seem to know, so I gave her directions to the March Hare's house, because he is a close relation of the White Rabbit.
Defence 2:	What were your impressions of Alice?
Cheshire Cat:	I thought she was a very polite, well-mannered little girl.
Defence 2:	Thank you. No further questions, My Lord/My Lady.
Judge:	*(To Prosecution)* Do you wish to cross-examine this witness?
Prosecution 2:	No, My Lord/My Lady.
Judge:	*(To Cheshire Cat)* You may step down.
	(The Cheshire Cat returns to his/her seat in the courtroom.)
	(To Defence) You may call your last witness.
Defence 3:	We call the Mad Hatter, My Lord/My Lady.
	(The Mad Hatter enters the witness stand.)
Court Clerk:	*(Approaches the witness stand)* Do you swear to tell the truth, the whole truth, and nothing but the truth?
Mad Hatter:	I do.
Court Clerk:	State your name and address.
Mad Hatter:	I'm the Mad Hatter, and I live at 2 Tea Cosy Lane, Wonderland.
Court Clerk:	Thank you. You may be seated.
	(The Mad Hatter sits down in the witness stand. The Court Clerk returns to his/her seat.)

Defence 3:	Mr. Mad Hatter, would you please describe how you met the defendant Alice.
Mad Hatter:	Certainly. My friends and I, the March Hare and the Dormouse, were having a tea party on April 1st. Alice suddenly came out of the woods and sat down at the table with us.
Defence 3:	What did you do then?
Mad Hatter:	We decided to celebrate Alice's unbirthday.
Defence 3:	Was she pleased?
Mad Hatter:	Well, I think so. She thought it was a curious idea. Then we started telling riddles. When she realized we didn't know any of the answers, she went off in search of the White Rabbit again.
Defence 3:	Did you mind that Alice had joined your tea party without being invited?
Mad Hatter:	If she hadn't, how would we have been able to celebrate her unbirthday?
Defence 3:	I take that to be no, then. Thank you, Mr. Hatter. No further questions, My Lord/My Lady.
Judge:	*(To Prosecution)* Do you wish to cross-examine this witness?
Prosecution 3:	Yes, My Lord/My Lady.
	Mr. Mad Hatter, were you the person giving this tea party?
Mad Hatter:	Well, no. It was at the home of the March Hare, so I suppose it was his party.
Prosecution 3:	Don't you think it was rather rude for Alice to sit down at a tea party to which she hadn't even been invited?
Defence 3:	My Lord/My Lady, I object! This calls for a conclusion on the part of the witness.
Judge:	Objection overruled. We need an answer to this question, but watch how you ask it. Please answer the question.

Mad Hatter:	No, we don't have many rules of that kind in Wonderland. Or rules of any kind, actually.
Prosecution 3:	No further questions, My Lord/My Lady.
Judge:	*(To Mad Hatter)* You may step down.
	(The Mad Hatter returns to his seat in the courtroom.)
Defence 3:	We rest our case, My Lord/My Lady.
Judge	*(To Defence)* You may begin your summation.
Defence 3:	Thank you, My Lord/My Lady.

(Closing statement) Ladies and gentlemen of the Jury, we have shown that Alice followed the White Rabbit into Wonderland only because she was curious. She did not mean to disturb anyone in Wonderland – in fact, you have heard testimony from two witnesses who have vouched for her enjoyable company and manners. The disturbance in the rose garden for which she is charged was no fault of hers, as it was due to a malfunction of her croquet equipment.

In fact, it is quite possible that this malfunction was created as a distraction by the Knave of Hearts.

Regarding the charge of theft, it was quite understandable that Alice ate the White Rabbit's cookies because she was hungry and to relieve the unpleasant circumstances brought about by her large size – not out of mischief. Therefore, we are certain that you will agree that Alice is innocent of both charges and will find her not guilty.

Judge:	*(To Defence)* Thank you.
	The Prosecution may now make its closing statement to the Jury.
Prosecution 3:	Thank you, My Lord/My Lady.

(Closing statement) Ladies and gentlemen of the Jury, we have shown that Alice followed the White Rabbit into Wonderland, where she had no right to go. Once there, she upset the inhabitants, took food and

drink that was not hers, deliberately disrupted and ruined the Queen of Hearts' croquet party. It should be no excuse that she didn't know the rules in Wonderland. She must be taught that it does not pay to be so curious!

We also argue that as she had no way of knowing that the White Rabbit's currant cookies would cause her to shrink, this should not be a valid defence for her theft of the cookies. She has demonstrated no remorse for either disturbance. We ask, therefore, that you find her guilty of both charges.

Judge:	*(To Prosecution)* Thank you.

(To Jury) As members of the Jury, you will have to make a decision of whether Alice is guilty or not guilty for each charge.

Alice stands charged that she:

"Did cause a disturbance in or near a public place, namely the Queen of Hearts' garden, by fighting and shouting, contrary to section 175(1) of *The Criminal Code of Canada*.

"Did steal a box of currant cookies, the property of the White Rabbit, of a value not exceeding $5 000, contrary to section 334(b) of *The Criminal Code of Canada*.

Think about what the witnesses and lawyers said during the trial. Your job is to carefully weigh the evidence from the both the prosecution and defence witnesses and lawyers and come to a decision. You need to decide which witnesses are more believable and which argument is most plausible. You will then vote on each charge. For this trial, your Jury is only required to reach a majority decision.

You now have 15 minutes to discuss the case. When you return, I will ask your Foreperson your verdict.

This is a suggested script only. Judges can feel free to elaborate.

Sheriff 2:	Order in the court. All rise.
	(Everyone stands.)
Court Clerk:	Court will now adjourn for 15 minutes.
	(The Judge and Jury leave the courtroom, followed by Sheriff 2.)
	(When the Judge and Jury are ready to return, approximately 15 minutes later, Sheriff 2 enters the courtroom and calls the court to order.)
Sheriff 2:	Order in the court. All rise.

	(Everyone stands as the Jury and then the Judge enter the courtroom and are seated.)
Court Clerk:	Court is now resumed. Please be seated.
	(All participants sit.)
Judge:	Mr./Madam Foreperson, have you reached a verdict?
Foreperson:	*(Stands)* Yes, My Lord/My Lady.
Judge:	Will the defendant please rise?
	(Alice and Sheriff 1 stand.)
Judge:	*(To Foreperson)* You may read the verdict.
Foreperson:	We find the accused, Alice, guilty/not guilty of the charge of disturbing the peace, and guilty/not guilty of the charge of theft under $5 000.
Judge:	Thank you.
	(The Judge then passes sentence if Alice is found guilty of either charge, or acquits Alice if she is found not guilty of all charges.)
Sheriff 1:	*(Standing)* Order in the court. All rise.
	(All participants stand.)
Court Clerk:	This court is now adjourned.